Copyright © Black Rise Limited, 2024

All rights reserved.

The moral rights of the authors have been asserted. No part of this work may be reproduced, stored in a retrieval system, or transmitted in any form or by any means, electronic, mechanical, photocopying, recording, or otherwise, without prior written permission from the publisher, except in the case of brief quotations embodied in critical articles or reviews.

The stories shared in this book are works of fiction, inspired by our research & analysis and the conversations on the Black Rise podcast. Names, characters, places, and incidents in the stories are either the product of imagination or used in a fictional manner. Any resemblance to actual persons, living or dead, events, or locales is entirely coincidental.

Illustrations copyright © 2024 by Black Rise Limited

Acknowledgements

We would like to extend our deepest gratitude to the incredible Black Leaders of the Black Rise podcast, whose stories, authenticity, and resilience have been a continuous source of inspiration for this book. Their voices have uplifted and empowered many, and we hope that their words will echo far and wide, carrying the strength of their journeys to all who need to hear them.

We extend our sincere gratitude to the visionary investors who believed in our mission from the start. Your trust and belief in our vision for Black Rise have been pivotal in making this journey possible. Your contributions have not only fueled our growth but also strengthened the foundation upon which we continue to build a thriving community and business ecosystem. Thank you for your unwavering support and commitment to fostering innovation and progress.

A heartfelt thank you to the Black Rise community for their unwavering support in bringing this project to life. Your collaboration and belief in our mission have been instrumental.

We would also like to recognise our creative team behind this work, whose dedication and passion have shaped every aspect of it. Lastly, to our friends and family for their love, patience, and unwavering encouragement—thank you from the bottom of our hearts.

Preface

Navigating the business world is much like playing a game of chess—strategic, thoughtful, and demanding. Throughout my journey, I have realised that success in your career is not simply about hard work; it's about knowing the rules of the game, anticipating your moves, and positioning yourself in ways that give you the advantage to win. The path to leadership, especially for Black professionals and entrepreneurs, requires more than just talent. It demands a strategic mindset, relentless determination, and the ability to make bold moves even when the odds seem stacked against you.

Win the Career Chess Game is a guide born out of my personal experiences, the lessons learned from countless setbacks, and the wisdom shared by the incredible leaders who have been part of my life. In this book, we lay out practical strategies for not just surviving but thriving in your career—turning every challenge into an opportunity and every "no" into a stepping stone toward the ultimate "yes."

This book is more than a series of tips and strategies; it's a call to action for those ready to take control of their careers, no matter where they are in their journey. Whether you are at the early stages or preparing for your next big move, the lessons within these pages will help you master the game of business and career advancement, ensuring you not only survive but emerge victorious.

As you read through the following chapters, I invite you to approach each lesson as a strategic move in your personal and professional game. Reflect on how you can implement these strategies to position yourself for success, build meaningful connections, and create opportunities not just for yourself but for others in your community. Winning the career chess game is about more than individual triumph; it's about reshaping the board so that future generations can play to win as well.

Thank you for joining me on this journey. Let's get ready to make bold moves and create a future where we all thrive.

With determination and purpose,

Flavilla Fongang

Founder of Black Rise

Contents

The Journey to Generational Wealth	2
Section 1: The Legacy of Wealth Inequality	6
Section 2: Overcoming Systemic Challenges	12
Section 3: Building Wealth through Education and Skill Development	14
Section 4: Entrepreneurship as a Wealth-Building Tool	20
Section 5: Investment and Financial Planning	26
Section 6: Community Wealth Building	32
Section 7: Legacy Building and Passing Wealth to Future Generations	38
Section 8: Inspiration from Black Wealth Builders	44
Flexible Task Plan for Building Generational Wealth	52
Conclusion of this guide: Moving Forward with Purpose	58
Chapter 01. The Power of Empathy and Continuous Learning in Leadership	61
Chapter 02. Building Resilience, Strategies for Entrepreneurial Success	63
Chapter 03. The Power of Building Advocacy and Sponsorship for Career Growth	65
Chapter 04. The Power of Strategic Networking and Value Creation	67
Chapter 05. The Power of Resilience and Strategic Focus in Entrepreneurship	69
Chapter 06. Navigating Change and Seizing Opportunities in a Career Path	71
Chapter 07. The Power of Strategic Collaboration for Growth in Business	73
Chapter 08. The Power of Networking and Human Connection in Business Success	75
Chapter 09. The Power of Niche Mastery and Strategic Alliances in Scaling a Business	77
Chapter 10. The Power of Resilience and Adaptability in Leadership	79
Chapter 11. Turning Frustration into Opportunity for Adaptability and Growth	81
Chapter 12. The Power of Strategic Partnerships and Willingness to Learn in Entrepreneurship	83
Chapter 13. Navigating the Complexities of Identity and Success	85
Chapter 14. Mastering the Art of Strategic Growth Beyond the Basics	87
Chapter 15. Building Your Career Chessboard - Strategic Moves for Long-Term Success	89
Chapter 16. Embracing Discomfort for Growth and Innovation	91
Chapter 17. The Power of Character and Resilience in Business Success	93
Chapter 18. The Power of Resilience and Strategic Patience in Career Advancement	95
Chapter 19. The Path to Business Growth and Success	97
Chapter 20. The Strategic Advantage of Content Driven Growth	99
Chapter 21. The Power of Strategic Networking and Continuous Learning in Business Success	101
Chapter 22. The Power of Strategic Patience in Career Advancement	103
Chapter 23. The Power of Persistence and Planning in Business Growth	105
Chapter 24. Leveraging Unconventional Opportunities for Career Growth	107

Chapter 25. A Strategic Approach to Success and Building Confidence	109
Chapter 26. Understanding Your Customers and Target Audience for Business Success	111
Chapter 27. The Power of Resilience and Adaptability in Leadership	113
Chapter 28. Harnessing Diverse Skills for Career Growth and Direction	115
Chapter 29. The Power of Adaptability and Agility in Navigating Business Challenges	117
Chapter 30. The Confidence Equation to Lead with Certainty in Uncertain Times	119
Chapter 31. Making Bold Moves to Cultivate Courage and Lead in Uncharted Waters	121
Chapter 32. The Role of Innovation in Future-Proofing Your Business	123
Chapter 33. Building Teams that Bring Their A-Game Every Day	125
Chapter 34. Embracing Failure as Fuel and Turning Setbacks into Springboards for Success	127
Chapter 35. Leading with Vision and Crafting a Strategy That Speaks to the Future	129
Chapter 36. The Power of Quiet Leadership to Inspire Through Action, Not Words	131
Chapter 37. From Ideas to Execution to Bridge the Gap with Strategic Clarity	133
Chapter 38. Daring to be Different and the Competitive Advantage of Diversity in Thought	135
Chapter 39. Seizing Opportunities you Didn't Plan for in Business	137
Chapter 40. Breaking Through the Noise and Standing Out in a Saturated Market	139
Chapter 41. Scaling with Intention and Avoiding Growth for Growth's Sake	141
Chapter 42. The Power of Purpose-Driven Leadership to Align Profit with Impact	143
Chapter 43. Mastering the Pivot and Knowing When and How to Change Direction	145
Chapter 44. Future-Proofing Your Leadership and Staying Ahead of Industry Disruption	147
Chapter 45. The Invisible Force of Culture as a Strategic Asset	149
Chapter 46. Building Bridges, Not Walls in Cross-Industry Collaboration	151
Chapter 47. Empowering and Elevating Others to Drive Collective Success	153
Chapter 48. The Power of Strategic Foresight to Anticipate Trends Before They Happen	155
Chapter 49. Unlocking Global Opportunities for Growth Beyond Boarders	157
Chapter 50. The Art of Reflection to Learn from Every Chapter in Your Leadership Journey	159
Chapter 51. Rewriting the Playbook and How to Lead When There Are No Rules	161
Chapter 52. Strategic Storytelling to Build a Narrative That Drives Action	163
Chapter 53. Building Legacy Leadership and Leading with a Future-First Mindset	165
Chapter 54. The Art of Graceful Leadership to Balance Strength with Compassion	167
Chapter 55. Unlocking the Power of Ecosystems to Leverage Partnerships for Growth	169
Chapter 56. Building Resilience for Sustained Success in Business	171
Chapter 57. How Small Wins Lead to Big Breakthroughs with the Multiplier Effect	173
Chapter 58. Unleashing the Power of Influence to Lead Without Authority	175
Chapter 59. Finding Your Strategic North Star for the Guiding Principles of Longterm Success	177
Be Part of Black Rise	179

Are you ready?

The Journey to Generational Wealth

What Is Generational Wealth?

Generational wealth refers to the assets passed down from one generation to the next. This can include anything of financial value—stocks, bonds, real estate, businesses, or even intellectual property. More than just material possessions, generational wealth represents a legacy of security, opportunity, and influence that can uplift future generations.

For Black professionals and entrepreneurs, building generational wealth carries additional layers of significance. Historically marginalised and systemically excluded from many avenues of wealth creation, Black communities have often faced unique challenges in creating and sustaining wealth. Despite these barriers, there has always been a deep-seated ambition within Black families and communities to foster success, uplift one another, and secure financial futures for generations to come.

Why Is Building Wealth Important in the Black Community?

Wealth is not merely about personal comfort or material success; it is a powerful tool for freedom and self-determination. Building generational wealth within the Black community can address long-standing economic inequalities, close the racial wealth gap, and create opportunities that were previously unavailable.

- **Economic Mobility:** Wealth allows individuals and families to rise above their circumstances, breaking cycles of poverty. For the Black community, this means creating lasting change that impacts entire communities, providing opportunities for homeownership, business development, and education.
- **Security and Stability:** With wealth comes financial security. Families with generational wealth can weather economic downturns, unexpected crises, and career changes without falling into financial hardship. This stability provides peace of mind and allows future generations to pursue higher education, start businesses, and live more comfortably.
- **Political and Social Influence:** Wealth provides a platform for political and social power. When communities have financial resources, they can influence policies, invest in advocacy efforts, and contribute to causes that further justice and equality.
- **Closing the Wealth Gap:** The racial wealth gap is a glaring economic disparity between Black and white households. By building generational wealth, Black families are taking direct action to close this gap, ensuring that future generations inherit not only money but also access to opportunities previously denied.

The Challenges Black Professionals and Entrepreneurs Face

The journey to generational wealth for Black professionals and entrepreneurs is riddled with obstacles that stem from systemic racism, lack of access to capital, and deep-rooted inequities in the financial system.

- **Historical Exclusion:** From redlining in real estate to Jim Crow laws and exclusion from certain industries, Black people have historically been denied access to wealth-building opportunities. This legacy of exclusion means that Black families often start from a place of financial disadvantage.
- **Limited Access to Capital:** Whether starting a business or purchasing a home, access to capital is key to wealth building. Yet Black entrepreneurs face significant challenges when seeking business loans, venture capital, or other funding. This is often due to discriminatory lending practices or a lack of connections within financial networks.

- **Systemic Barriers:** Even in corporate settings, Black professionals encounter glass ceilings, wage disparities, and fewer opportunities for advancement compared to their white counterparts. This limits earning potential and the ability to accumulate wealth.
- **Financial Literacy Gaps:** Due to the generational effects of exclusion from wealth-building systems, financial literacy within Black communities can sometimes lag. Many individuals are not taught about investing, savings, credit management, or estate planning at the same rate as other communities. Closing this knowledge gap is crucial for financial empowerment.

Purpose of This Book

This book is designed as a roadmap to help you navigate the complexities of wealth building. Through a combination of education, strategy, and inspiration, we seek you to empower, our readers, with the tools needed to create a lasting financial legacy.

Key Themes to Expect:

- **Education:** Learning the historical context and systemic challenges unique to the Black community is essential for understanding the journey to generational wealth.
- **Strategic Planning:** Practical steps and strategies, from entrepreneurship to investment planning, will provide readers with actionable ways to begin building and preserving wealth.
- **Inspiration:** Through case studies and real-life stories of Black professionals and entrepreneurs who have successfully created wealth, this book will offer motivation and a sense of possibility.
- **Community Empowerment:** Building wealth isn't just an individual pursuit. This book will also explore the importance of community wealth-building and how collective efforts can have a lasting impact on future generations.
- The book ends with 59 fictional business stories with key action points that you can apply right away.

Introducing the Black Wealth-Building Framework

At the heart of this book is the **Black Wealth-Building Framework**—a step-by-step guide that outlines a clear path to creating generational wealth. This framework acknowledges the unique barriers faced by Black individuals while offering strategies to overcome them. The seven steps in the framework include:

1. **Awareness and Education:** Understand the historical and social landscape of wealth inequality.
2. **Strategic Action:** Develop a wealth-building strategy through career growth and entrepreneurship.
3. **Accessing Capital and Resources:** Identify and secure funding sources and networks.
4. **Investment and Asset Building:** Accumulate assets and manage investments wisely.
5. **Family Legacy Planning:** Ensure wealth is passed down through generations by preparing legally and educating your family.
6. **Community Wealth Building:** Support and grow wealth within your community.
7. **Consistency, Patience, and Adaptation:** Embrace a long-term approach to wealth-building, staying resilient through challenges.

Each section of this guide corresponds to a step in this framework, breaking down the complexities of wealth building into manageable, actionable tasks. Whether you're at the beginning of your career or already a seasoned entrepreneur, this will serve as your guide in the journey toward creating a lasting legacy.

Section 1: The Legacy of Wealth Inequality

Historical Barriers to Wealth Creation for Black Communities in the UK and Europe

The history of Black communities in the UK and Europe is deeply intertwined with colonialism, the transatlantic slave trade, and systemic exclusion from economic opportunities. While the legacy of slavery shaped Black wealth inequality in the U.S., in the U.K. and Europe, colonialism and immigration have played key roles in creating and perpetuating economic disparities for Black individuals.

1.1 The Impact of Colonialism on Wealth Building

The transatlantic slave trade, largely financed and profited from by European powers such as the UK, France, Portugal, and the Netherlands, had devastating effects on Africa, stripping the continent of its human resources and wealth. Although slavery as an institution was not as embedded in the daily lives of European countries as in the U.S., European economies thrived on the exploitation of African labour and resources through colonialism.

The wealth extracted from African colonies, and the Caribbean, where enslaved Africans were forced to work, enriched European nations, banks, and aristocratic families while leaving African and Caribbean countries economically weakened. This colonial legacy continues to affect the economic position of Black immigrants in Europe today.

For example, after the UK abolished slavery in 1833, the British government compensated slave owners rather than the enslaved, distributing £20 million (approximately £17 billion today) to wealthy families. These funds further entrenched generational wealth for white British families, while Black people in the Caribbean and Africa received nothing. Many descendants of these wealthy families continue to benefit from inherited wealth, while Black individuals in the UK are still dealing with the long-term effects of systemic economic exclusion.

1.2 Housing Discrimination and Segregation in the UK and Europe

In the UK, the arrival of the **Windrush Generation** (Caribbean immigrants invited to help rebuild post-war Britain) was met with systemic discrimination in housing. Black Britons were often forced into low-quality, overcrowded housing due to racial prejudice from landlords and housing authorities. Similar forms of segregation and discrimination existed in countries like France and the Netherlands, where Black immigrants from Africa and the Caribbean were pushed to live in poorer, marginalised neighbourhoods.

In the UK, **race relations legislation** was introduced to combat discrimination, but disparities persist. Housing remains a significant barrier to wealth building for Black Britons, who are less likely to own homes compared to their white counterparts. According to a 2020 UK government report, **68% of white households** own their homes, compared to only **20% of Black African households**. Homeownership is a key factor in wealth-building, and this disparity directly contributes to the racial wealth gap.

In France, the banlieues (suburbs) surrounding major cities such as Paris have become a symbol of the systemic exclusion of Black and North African immigrants. These areas are often underfunded, over-policed, and lacking in economic opportunity. The inability to access better housing and quality public services has long-term effects on wealth-building for Black communities in France and other European countries with similar dynamics, such as Belgium and the Netherlands.

1.3 Employment Discrimination in the UK and Europe

Employment has been another critical area where Black professionals and entrepreneurs face systemic challenges. In the UK, studies have shown that Black workers are less likely to be hired, promoted, or paid equally compared to white workers, even when they possess the same qualifications.

According to research by the **Institute for Public Policy Research (IPPR)**, Black Britons are more than **twice as likely to be unemployed** as their white counterparts. Even when employed, the pay gap remains significant. A 2021 study found that Black employees in the UK earn on average **16% less** than white workers. This pay disparity makes it more difficult for Black individuals to save, invest, and build wealth.

In France, employment discrimination against Black and North African communities has been well-documented. According to research from the **French National Institute of Statistics and Economic Studies (INSEE)**, Black workers face significantly higher rates of unemployment and are often paid less than their white colleagues. The combination of employment discrimination and limited career advancement opportunities further exacerbates the wealth gap for Black individuals in Europe.

The Racial Wealth Gap: Facts and Figures in the UK and Europe

The racial wealth gap is just as pervasive in the UK and Europe as it is in the U.S., although it is often less publicly acknowledged. While income inequality is a contributing factor, the wealth gap is largely a result of generational exclusion from wealth-building opportunities such as homeownership, investments, and entrepreneurship.

1.4 Data on the Racial Wealth Gap

In the UK, the Resolution Foundation published a 2020 report showing that Black African and Caribbean households are far more likely to live in poverty than white households, and homeownership rates among Black households are significantly lower. Only **20% of Black African households** own their homes, compared to nearly **70% of white British households**.

In France, wealth disparities between Black and white citizens are also stark, though not as thoroughly studied. Black and immigrant families are disproportionately represented in low-income neighbourhoods, with limited access to financial services, education, and employment. The systematic exclusion of Black individuals from high-paying jobs and wealth-building opportunities continues to widen the wealth gap.

1.5 Root Causes of the Wealth Gap in the UK and Europe

Some of the primary factors contributing to the racial wealth gap in the UK and Europe include:

- **Homeownership Disparities:** In the UK, Black households are far less likely to own property than white households. Homeownership is one of the most important drivers of wealth accumulation, and being denied access to mortgages or affordable housing has limited the ability of Black families to build wealth.
- **Educational Inequalities:** Access to education plays a critical role in wealth-building, but Black students in the UK and Europe often face barriers to higher education. In the UK, Black students are disproportionately represented in lower-ranking universities and have higher levels of student debt. This limits their long-term earning potential, as top-tier education often leads to better-paying jobs.
- **Employment Discrimination:** The pay gap and employment discrimination faced by Black workers across Europe limits their ability to save, invest, and build wealth. Black professionals often have to work harder for the same opportunities as their white counterparts, facing both explicit and implicit racial bias in the workplace.

- **Generational Poverty:** Many Black families in the UK and Europe have experienced generational poverty, exacerbated by systemic discrimination in employment, housing, and education. This makes it difficult to accumulate wealth over time.

Addressing Financial Literacy Gaps in Black Communities in the UK and Europe

Closing the financial literacy gap is crucial for Black professionals and entrepreneurs in the UK and Europe. Financial education equips individuals with the tools to make informed decisions about saving, investing, and planning for their financial futures.

1.6 Why Financial Literacy Is Essential

In the UK and Europe, financial literacy is not evenly distributed, and Black communities are often left out of wealth-building conversations. Teaching financial literacy in schools, workplaces, and communities is essential for equipping individuals with the knowledge needed to make smart financial decisions. Black professionals and entrepreneurs must understand the nuances of saving, budgeting, credit management, investing, and estate planning to build long-term wealth.

1.7 Strategies for Improving Financial Literacy

There are several resources and organisations in the UK and Europe working to address financial literacy within Black communities:

- **Black Rise** connects Black professionals and entrepreneurs so they can share knowledge and expertise
- **The Black Business Network** in the UK offers educational resources and mentorship for Black entrepreneurs looking to build wealth.
- **Black Economics** UK provides insights into the economic position of Black communities in the UK and offers educational programs to improve financial literacy.
- Across Europe, organisations like the **African Diaspora Network in Europe (ADNE)** and **Africa-Europe Diaspora Development Platform (ADEPT)** work to promote financial literacy and entrepreneurship among Black communities.

By taking advantage of these resources, as a Black individual, you can develop the skills needed to navigate the complex world of personal finance and business development.

The legacy of wealth inequality for Black individuals in the UK and Europe is deeply rooted in colonialism, immigration policies, and systemic exclusion from economic opportunities. From discriminatory housing practices to employment bias, Black communities have long been denied the same pathways to wealth as their white counterparts. Understanding these historical barriers is essential for addressing them and taking proactive steps toward wealth-building.

Section 2: Overcoming Systemic Challenges

2.1 Systemic Racism in the UK and Europe

Systemic racism in the UK and Europe manifests in different ways than in the U.S., but it remains a significant barrier to wealth creation. In the UK, Black professionals are less likely to be promoted to senior positions, and racial bias in hiring is a persistent issue. A study by **The Guardian** revealed that **Black graduates in the UK earn 23% less** on average than their white counterparts, even when they have similar qualifications.

In Europe, systemic racism is particularly prevalent in countries like France, where the treatment of Black people is deeply tied to the legacy of colonialism. Discrimination in employment, housing, and education has long hindered the economic mobility of Black Europeans. In the Netherlands, Black Dutch citizens, particularly those of African and Caribbean descent, face similar barriers in the workforce and housing markets.

2.1.1 Navigating Systemic Racism in the Workplace (UK and Europe)

- **UK Strategies:** As a Black professional in the UK, you can leverage networks such as **The Black British Business Awards**, which focus on supporting Black leadership and entrepreneurship. These organisations provide mentorship, networking, and visibility, which are essential for career advancement
- **European Strategies:** Across Europe, initiatives like **Diaspora RiseUp** and **The European Network Against Racism (ENAR)** work to tackle racial discrimination in the workplace and provide resources for Black professionals to navigate systemic racism.

2.2 Disparities in Access to Capital (UK and Europe)

In the UK, Black entrepreneurs face significant challenges when trying to secure funding. According to a report by **Extend Ventures**, between 2009 and 2019, just **0.24%** of venture capital invested in UK startups went to Black entrepreneurs. Similarly, banks in the UK are less likely to approve loans for Black business owners, creating a barrier to scaling their enterprises.

In Europe, Black entrepreneurs face similar hurdles, with limited access to venture capital and discriminatory lending practices. Many European countries lack formal networks for minority-focused funding, further restricting access to capital for Black entrepreneurs.

2.2.1 Strategies to Access Capital (UK and Europe)

- **UK Solutions:** Black entrepreneurs in the UK can explore initiatives like **The UK Black Business Fund** or **Colorintech**, which are focused on providing funding and resources to Black-owned startups. Additionally, **The Prince's Trust** offers support for young Black entrepreneurs.
- **European Solutions:** In Europe, programs like **ADEPT (African Diaspora Entrepreneurship Program)** and the **Black-owned business collective, UMOJA** provide mentorship, resources, and investment opportunities for Black entrepreneurs across the continent.

Section 3: Building Wealth through Education and Skill Development

Education and skill development are among the most powerful tools for building wealth and breaking the cycle of generational poverty. In the UK and Europe, access to quality education and vocational training can open doors to higher-paying jobs, entrepreneurial success, and long-term wealth creation. However, systemic barriers have historically limited Black individuals' access to the same educational and professional opportunities as their white counterparts.

In this section, we'll discuss how you can leverage education to increase your earning potential, develop marketable skills, and position yourself for long-term success. We'll also explore the importance of mentorship, lifelong learning, and vocational training.

3.1 The Power of Education in Closing the Wealth Gap

Education is a critical wealth-building tool for individuals and families. Higher levels of education are strongly correlated with higher earning potential, better job opportunities, and access to wealth-building strategies like investing and homeownership. For Black professionals and entrepreneurs in the UK and Europe, achieving educational equity is essential for closing the racial wealth gap.

3.1.1 Disparities in Educational Access

In the UK, Black students are disproportionately represented in lower-performing schools and are less likely to attend elite universities compared to their white peers. Data from the **Department for Education** reveals that Black Caribbean students are significantly less likely to achieve top GCSE and A-Level results, which limits their access to top-tier universities and higher-paying career paths.

Once in higher education, Black students in the UK face additional challenges. The **2019 Office for Students** report found that Black students are more likely to drop out of university, less likely to graduate with a first or upper-second-class degree, and more likely to leave school with significant student debt. This educational disadvantage has long-term effects on earning potential and wealth accumulation.

In Europe, similar trends can be seen. In France, for example, students of African descent often attend underfunded schools in marginalised suburbs, with limited access to higher education. According to research by **Institut Montaigne**, students of African and Caribbean descent face barriers to entering prestigious universities and professional sectors, which limits their access to high-paying jobs.

3.1.2 Overcoming Educational Barriers

To build wealth through education, Black professionals and entrepreneurs in the UK and Europe must actively seek out opportunities for learning and development, despite systemic barriers. Here are some strategies to overcome these challenges:

- **Scholarships and Financial Support:** In the UK, scholarships and bursaries are available for Black students at universities such as **Oxford** and **Cambridge**, as well as through organisations like **The Black Heart Foundation** and **The Amos Bursary**. In Europe, organisations like **ADEPT** and **Africa-France** offer financial support for Black students pursuing higher education.
- **Mentorship Programs:** Mentorship plays a crucial role in helping Black students navigate the education system and career pathways. Programs like **SEO London** and **Target Oxbridge** in the UK provide mentorship and guidance for Black students aiming for elite universities and professional sectors.
- **Vocational Training and Apprenticeships:** For those who do not pursue traditional academic routes, vocational training and apprenticeships offer alternative pathways to high-paying careers. In the UK, organisations like **Black Training and Enterprise Group (BTEG)** work to provide access to apprenticeships and job training for Black youth. In Germany and other European countries, vocational training systems are well-established, offering Black individuals opportunities to gain skills in trades and technical fields.

3.2 Lifelong Learning and Skill Development

In an increasingly dynamic and globalised economy, the ability to continuously develop new skills is essential for career growth and wealth-building. Whether you are a professional seeking to climb the corporate ladder or an entrepreneur aiming to scale your business, staying current with industry trends and expanding your skillset will significantly improve your earning potential.

3.2.1 Upskilling for Career Advancement

For Black professionals, career advancement can be hindered by racial bias and glass ceilings. However, developing in-demand skills can help you overcome these barriers by increasing your marketability and opening doors to higher-paying positions.

Key areas of skill development include:

- **Digital Skills:** With the rapid growth of the tech sector, acquiring digital skills such as coding, data analysis, and digital marketing can significantly increase earning potential. In the UK, initiatives like **Colorintech** focus on helping Black individuals break into the tech industry, providing training and mentorship.
- **Leadership and Management:** Developing leadership and management skills is critical for career progression. Black professionals should seek out opportunities for leadership training, such as **MBA programs**, executive education courses, and mentorship in management roles. Many universities and organisations, including **The London Business School**, offer scholarships to support Black students in pursuing advanced degrees in leadership.
- **Soft Skills:** Communication, negotiation, and networking skills are vital for advancing in any career. These skills can help Black professionals navigate workplace dynamics, negotiate salaries, and secure promotions.

3.2.2 Lifelong Learning for Entrepreneurs

Entrepreneurship is a powerful vehicle for wealth creation, but it requires continuous learning and adaptation to stay competitive. You should prioritise learning about business strategy, financial management, and marketing to grow and scale their businesses.

Resources for continuous learning include:

- **Business Accelerators and Incubators:** Programs like **Foundervine** in the UK and Startupbootcamp in Europe offer business accelerators and incubators specifically designed to support underrepresented entrepreneurs, including Black founders. These programs provide mentorship, training, and networking opportunities.
- **Online Courses and Certifications:** Platforms like **Coursera, LinkedIn Learning**, and **Udemy** offer courses in entrepreneurship, finance, marketing, and leadership. You can use these platforms to acquire new skills that will help you manage and grow their businesses more effectively.
- **Networking and Business Communities:** Joining organisations such as **The Black Business Network (UK)** or **The African Business Chamber (AFRICAB)** in Europe can provide access to workshops, seminars, and peer support for Black entrepreneurs.

3.3 Leveraging Mentorship and Community Support

Mentorship and community support are essential for wealth-building, particularly for Black professionals and entrepreneurs who often lack access to the same networks and resources as their white counterparts. By tapping into existing networks and mentorship opportunities, you can gain invaluable insights, connections, and guidance on how to navigate your careers and businesses.

3.3.1 The Importance of Mentorship

Mentorship provides the guidance and support needed to overcome challenges, develop skills, and achieve professional goals. A mentor can offer advice on career decisions, provide feedback on business strategies, and open doors to new opportunities. Mentorship is particularly important in overcoming systemic barriers and navigating industries where For Black professionals and entrepreneurs are underrepresented.

Programs like **The Aleto Foundation** in the UK and **The African Diaspora Network in Europe (ADNE)** connect Black individuals with experienced professionals and business leaders who can offer mentorship and support.

3.3.2 Building and Utilising Networks

In addition to mentorship, building a strong professional network is crucial for career growth and business success. Networking can lead to job opportunities, partnerships, and access to resources that can accelerate wealth-building.

Joining networks like **Black Rise, The Black British Business Awards, The Association of Black Business Owners and Professionals (ABBP)**, or **Black Professionals Scotland** can provide you access to events, workshops, and networking opportunities that are designed to support you.

Education and skill development are foundational elements of wealth-building. By overcoming educational barriers, engaging in lifelong learning, and leveraging mentorship and community support, you can significantly improve your earning potential and create pathways to generational wealth. Whether through academic achievement, vocational training, or entrepreneurship, continuous learning and skill-building are essential for your long-term success.

Section 4: Entrepreneurship as a Wealth-Building Tool

Entrepreneurship has long been a pathway to wealth creation, offering individuals the opportunity to generate income, create jobs, and build lasting legacies. For Black professionals and entrepreneurs, business ownership can be a powerful tool to combat systemic barriers to wealth-building. However, the road to entrepreneurial success is often fraught with unique challenges, including limited access to funding, discrimination in business networks, and the pressures of sustaining a business in competitive markets.

In this section, we'll explore how Black entrepreneurs can navigate these challenges, identify profitable niches, and build resilient businesses that contribute to long-term wealth.

4.1 The Role of Entrepreneurship in Wealth-Building

Entrepreneurship offers a direct path to financial independence and wealth accumulation. For Black individuals, starting and growing a business can help bridge the racial wealth gap by providing opportunities to generate income, create assets, and pass down wealth to future generations.

However, entrepreneurship also involves risks, and Black entrepreneurs must navigate additional hurdles, such as discriminatory lending practices, limited access to venture capital, and exclusion from mainstream business networks.

4.1.1 Entrepreneurship as an Economic Equaliser

Owning a business allows individuals to have greater control over their financial futures and reduce reliance on traditional employment, where systemic racism and wage gaps are prevalent. Through entrepreneurship, Black individuals can build equity in their businesses, create additional revenue streams, and diversify their income. As businesses grow and succeed, they can also create employment opportunities within their communities, driving local economic growth.

- **Economic Independence:** By starting your own businesses, you can break free from employment barriers, achieve financial independence, and create wealth-building opportunities that are not subject to racial wage gaps.
- **Job Creation:** Black-owned businesses can uplift local economies by creating jobs and reinvesting in Black communities. This fosters economic empowerment on a larger scale and helps build collective wealth.
- **Legacy Building:** Entrepreneurship provides the opportunity to create businesses that can be passed down to future generations. Family-owned businesses can be a significant source of generational wealth.

4.1.2 Case Studies of Successful Black Entrepreneurs in the UK and Europe

- **Raphael Sofoluke** (UK): Founder of the **UK Black Business Show**, Sofoluke created an influential platform to celebrate and promote Black entrepreneurs. The success of the Black Business Show has helped highlight the power of Black business ownership in the UK and inspired a generation of entrepreneurs.
- **Yvonne Thompson CBE** (UK): An influential businesswoman and entrepreneur, Thompson is the founder of **Changing Faces**, a communications and marketing agency. She is also known for her work promoting diversity in the boardroom and entrepreneurship, inspiring countless Black professionals.
- **Alain Mabanckou** (France): A Congolese-French writer, entrepreneur, and public intellectual, Mabanckou has built a successful career in both literature and entrepreneurship. His work illustrates the possibilities of cross-disciplinary entrepreneurship, blending creative and business pursuits.

4.2 Identifying Profitable Niches and Building Resilient Businesses

As a Black entrepreneur, identifying profitable niches is essential for building successful businesses. It's important to understand market demand, leverage unique cultural insights, and create products or services that resonate with a targeted audience.

4.2.1 Leveraging Cultural Capital

One of the strengths Black entrepreneurs bring to the table is the ability to leverage cultural capital. Whether through products that cater to underrepresented communities or innovative services that reflect the cultural diversity, Black-owned businesses can tap into underserved markets.

- **Example:** The rise of Black-owned beauty brands such as **Afrocenchix** in the UK, which caters to the natural hair care market, demonstrates how Black entrepreneurs can successfully create businesses that serve the needs of their communities while capitalising on market gaps.
- **Example:** In France, entrepreneurs like **Fabrice Guerrier**, founder of **Syllble**, a collaborative community for creative writers of African descent, have created platforms that celebrate Black culture while building profitable businesses.

4.2.2 Conducting Market Research and Competitive Analysis

Conducting thorough market research and competitive analysis is key to identifying profitable niches. As entrepreneur, you should focus on understanding market trends, consumer behaviour, and the competitive landscape to determine the best areas to invest time and resources. Key steps include:

- **Understanding Demand:** Identifying consumer needs that are currently unmet or underserved.
- **Competitive Landscape:** Evaluating existing competitors and identifying what gaps or weaknesses can be exploited.
- **Innovative Products or Services:** Developing unique products or services that address specific pain points or cater to niche audiences.

You can use government resources such as the **UK Government's Business** and **Enterprise Support** programs or EU initiatives to conduct market research, receive advice on business development, and access mentorship.

4.3 Overcoming Funding Challenges

Access to capital is one of the most significant challenges Black entrepreneurs face when starting and scaling their businesses. Traditional banks, venture capital firms, and investors have historically overlooked Black entrepreneurs, offering fewer loans, stricter repayment terms, or smaller investment amounts compared to their white counterparts.

4.3.1 Funding Sources for Black Entrepreneurs in the UK and Europe

- **Grants and Government Support:** In the UK, programs like **The Black Business Fund** and the **Prince's Trust Enterprise Program** offer grants, low-interest loans, and business development support to Black entrepreneurs. In Europe, the **European Investment Fund** provides resources to support minority entrepreneurs, particularly through initiatives aimed at fostering diversity in business.
- **Crowdfunding Platforms:** Black entrepreneurs can also turn to crowdfunding platforms like **Kickstarter**, **GoFundMe**, and **Seedrs** to raise capital. Crowdfunding allows entrepreneurs to bypass traditional financing routes by appealing directly to their customers and supporters for funding.
- **Angel Investors and Venture Capital:** While access to venture capital remains limited, there are emerging funds in the UK and Europe specifically aimed at investing in Black and minority-owned businesses. **Colorintech** and **Impact X Capital** in the UK are two examples

of organisations focused on funding Black tech entrepreneurs.
- **Microfinance and Peer-to-Peer Lending:** Microfinance institutions, such as **Kiva** and **Funding Circle**, offer smaller loans with favourable terms, making them more accessible for Black entrepreneurs who may struggle to secure larger loans from traditional banks.

4.3.2 Strategies for Securing Investment

To improve their chances of securing funding, Black entrepreneurs should consider the following strategies:

- **Develop a Strong Business Plan:** Investors and lenders need to see a well-thought-out business plan that clearly outlines the value proposition, target market, financial projections, and growth strategy. Black entrepreneurs should focus on crafting compelling business plans that highlight the potential for success.
- **Networking and Building Relationships:** Building relationships with potential investors and business mentors can open doors to funding opportunities. Attending industry events, pitch competitions, and networking events hosted by organisations like **Black Rise, The UK Black Business Show** or **AfriCaribbean Trade and Investment Forum** can be valuable opportunities to connect with funders.
- **Exploring Alternative Financing Options:** If traditional bank loans and venture capital funding are out of reach, Black entrepreneurs should explore other financing options, such as revenue-based financing, business accelerators, or equity crowdfunding platforms like **Crowdcube**.

4.4 Leveraging Technology and Innovation

In today's global marketplace, technology and innovation play a critical role in scaling businesses and staying competitive. As a Black entrepreneur, you can leverage digital tools to grow their businesses, reach wider audiences, and optimise operations.

4.4.1 E-Commerce and Digital Marketing

The shift toward e-commerce offers significant opportunities for Black entrepreneurs to scale their businesses online. By creating a strong online presence, utilising social media, and engaging in digital marketing strategies, entrepreneurs can reach global audiences and expand their customer base.

- **Example:** UK-based entrepreneur **Bianca Miller-Cole**, founder of **The Be Group**, successfully used digital platforms to promote her personal branding business and launch a line of inclusive hosiery that caters to women of all skin tones. Her business model highlights how leveraging technology can expand market reach.

4.4.2 Tech Startups and Innovation

In addition to traditional business models, Black entrepreneurs can explore opportunities in tech startups. The tech sector is rapidly growing in the UK and Europe, and programs like **Black Valley** and **Colorintech** offer mentorship, funding, and accelerator programs for Black tech entrepreneurs.

Black founders should focus on innovation in areas like fintech, health tech, and e-commerce, where there is significant growth potential. Leveraging technology not only improves operational efficiency but also creates scalable businesses that can generate wealth over the long term.

Entrepreneurship is a powerful wealth-building tool for Black professionals in the UK and Europe. By identifying profitable niches, overcoming funding challenges, and leveraging technology, Black entrepreneurs can build successful, resilient businesses that contribute to generational wealth. With the right resources, mentorship, and strategies, Black entrepreneurs can navigate systemic barriers and create long-lasting economic legacies.

Section 5: Investment and Financial Planning

Investment and financial planning are foundational elements in the journey to building generational wealth. Understanding how to make smart investment choices and develop a solid financial plan is crucial for your long-term wealth accumulation and asset protection.

This section will explore different investment opportunities and financial planning strategies, including real estate, stock market investments, business ownership, and retirement planning. By developing a diversified investment portfolio and making informed financial decisions, you can lay the groundwork for a financially secure future.

5.1 Key Investments that Promote Generational Wealth

When it comes to building wealth, making the right investments is critical. Investments provide the opportunity for long-term growth, allowing individuals to accumulate assets that appreciate over time and generate passive income. Some of the most important investment avenues include real estate, stocks, and business ownership.

5.1.1 Real Estate

Real estate is one of the most effective and accessible ways to build wealth. Property ownership offers multiple benefits, including long-term appreciation, rental income, and tax advantages. Owning property also provides an asset that can be passed down to future generations, creating a legacy of wealth.

- **Property Ownership in the UK:** The UK has a strong property market, particularly in cities like London, Birmingham, and Manchester. Buying property in areas with strong growth potential allows Black investors to build equity and generate rental income. Programs like **Help to Buy** and **Shared Ownership** can assist first-time buyers in getting onto the property ladder.
- **Real Estate in Europe:** In Europe, countries like France, Germany, and Spain also offer strong real estate investment opportunities. For example, in France, you can take advantage of relatively stable property prices and long-term appreciation in cities like Paris, Lyon, and Marseille. Similarly, Spain's real estate market, especially in tourist areas, presents opportunities for rental income and property appreciation.
- **Challenges and Strategies:** One challenge Black investors often face is limited access to affordable mortgage financing due to systemic bias in lending. You can work around this by leveraging government-backed schemes, exploring lower-cost property markets, and joining real estate investment groups to pool resources.

5.1.2 Stock Market Investments

The stock market is another essential tool for wealth-building. Investing in stocks offers the potential for significant returns over time, particularly when investments are held for the long term. You can take advantage of stock market opportunities through individual stock purchases, mutual funds, and exchange-traded funds (ETFs).

- **UK Stock Market:** The **FTSE 100** and **FTSE 250** indexes offer investment opportunities in some of the largest companies in the UK. By investing in these markets, you can diversify your portfolios and access growth in industries ranging from technology to finance.
- **European Stock Markets:** The **Euronext** exchange, which includes markets in France, Belgium, and the Netherlands, offers access to a wide range of stocks across European companies. By investing in industries such as manufacturing, renewable energy, and consumer goods, you can benefit from market growth.

5.1.3 Business Ownership

As discussed in Section 4, entrepreneurship is a critical wealth-building tool. Business ownership provides an opportunity to build a sustainable, income-generating enterprise that can grow in value over time. In addition to generating income, successful businesses can be sold for profit, expanded into new markets, or passed down to future generations.

Building a business with strong growth potential is essential for long-term wealth accumulation. Industries such as technology, e-commerce, real estate, and consulting are particularly lucrative areas for business ownership.

5.2 Building a Diversified Investment Portfolio

Diversification is a key principle of investment. By spreading investments across different asset classes, individuals can reduce risk and increase the likelihood of consistent returns. Creating a diversified portfolio is critical for managing financial risk and maximising growth opportunities.

5.2.1 Asset Classes for Diversification

- **Real Estate:** Property investments offer stability and long-term appreciation. Investors can hold residential or commercial properties, generating rental income or profits from property sales.
- **Stocks and Bonds:** Stock market investments provide exposure to high-growth industries, while bonds offer a safer, lower-risk option for generating steady returns. You should consider a mix of stocks and bonds to balance risk and reward.
- **Private Equity and Startups:** Investing in private equity or startups can offer high returns, particularly in emerging sectors such as technology and renewable energy. You can also explore crowdfunding platforms to invest in startups or new ventures.
- **Commodities:** Commodities like gold, oil, and agricultural products can serve as a hedge against inflation and provide portfolio diversification.

5.2.2 Tools for Managing Investments

To build and manage a diversified portfolio, Black investors in the UK and Europe can leverage investment platforms such as **Trading 212**, **Hargreaves Lansdown** and **Freetrade** in the UK, or **Degiro** and **Interactive Brokers** in Europe. These platforms offer access to a wide range of investments, including stocks, bonds, ETFs, and more.

Financial advisors and wealth management firms also provide support in creating and managing investment portfolios. You may benefit from working with advisors who specialise in minority wealth-building strategies, ensuring their investments align with long-term goals.

5.3 Wealth Management and Financial Advisors

Wealth management is essential for protecting and growing your assets over time. By working with financial advisors, you can create personalised financial plans that account for investment goals, risk tolerance, and long-term aspirations.

5.3.1 Choosing the Right Financial Advisor

Finding a financial advisor who understands your unique challenges is crucial. Look for advisors who are experienced in working with minority clients, understand the barriers to wealth-building, and can provide tailored investment strategies. Organisations such as the **Black Wealth Network** in the UK and the **African Diaspora Finance Network** in Europe can provide recommendations for culturally competent advisors.

5.3.2 Financial Planning for Retirement

A critical component of financial planning is preparing for retirement. You should ensure you are taking advantage of pension schemes, such as the **Workplace Pension** in the UK or equivalent retirement plans in European countries. Contributing to these schemes allows for tax-deferred growth and provides financial security in later years.

In addition, investing in personal pension plans, such as **Self-Invested Personal Pensions (SIPPs)** can provide more control over retirement investments and increase wealth accumulation.

5.4 Estate Planning and Asset Protection

Building wealth is only half the battle—ensuring it is preserved for future generations is equally important. Estate planning is a crucial part of generational wealth-building, as it ensures that assets are protected and transferred smoothly to heirs.

5.4.1 Creating Wills and Trusts

Creating a will or trust is essential for protecting wealth and avoiding disputes over inheritance. Wills clearly outline how assets should be distributed, while trusts can help protect assets from taxes and ensure they are passed down efficiently.

- **Trusts:** Setting up family trusts can help protect assets from probate and tax burdens. Trusts can also provide a way to manage wealth for future generations, ensuring that assets are used responsibly and preserved over time.
- **Inheritance Tax Planning:** In the UK, inheritance tax can significantly reduce the value of assets passed down to heirs. Proper tax planning can help minimise these costs, ensuring that more wealth is preserved for future generations.

5.4.2 Protecting Assets with Insurance

Another critical element of asset protection is insurance. You should consider life insurance, health insurance, and business insurance to protect your wealth in the event of unexpected life changes, health issues, or business risks. Insurance provides a financial safety net and ensures that your family members are taken care of in case of emergencies.

Investment and financial planning are at the core of building and preserving wealth. By making smart investments in real estate, the stock market, and businesses, and by managing a diversified portfolio, you can create lasting financial security. Proper wealth management, estate planning, and asset protection are critical for ensuring that your wealth is not only built but also passed down to future generations.

Section 6: Community Wealth Building

Wealth-building is not just an individual pursuit—it is also a collective endeavour that can uplift entire communities. Community wealth-building provides an opportunity to address systemic barriers, strengthen local economies, and ensure that wealth is distributed across generations. By working together to build financial resilience and support Black-owned businesses, as Black communities, we can create self-sustaining economic ecosystems that foster generational wealth.

In this section, we will explore the importance of community wealth-building and examine practical ways to invest in Black communities, support local businesses, and develop cooperative economic models.

6.1 The Power of Collective Wealth Building

Building generational wealth is not only about personal financial success but also about empowering the wider community. Community wealth-building is a powerful tool for combating the economic disparities that have resulted from centuries of exclusion and systemic racism.

6.1.1 Why Community Wealth Building Matters

- **Economic Empowerment:** Community wealth-building strengthens local economies by creating jobs, increasing business ownership, and fostering financial independence within Black communities. When wealth circulates within the community, it has a multiplier effect, benefiting more individuals and businesses.
- **Resilience Against Economic Shocks:** By building collective wealth, communities can create safety nets that protect against economic downturns and systemic challenges. Black communities that invest in shared resources and cooperative economics are better equipped to handle financial crises and ensure that wealth is preserved for future generations.
- **Social and Political Influence:** Economic power translates into social and political influence. Communities with strong financial foundations are more likely to advocate for policies that support economic justice, improve education, and promote social equality.

6.1.2 Historical Examples of Collective Wealth Building

Black communities throughout history have demonstrated the power of collective wealth-building, particularly in response to systemic exclusion. One notable example is **Black Wall Street** in Tulsa, Oklahoma (U.S.), which became a thriving economic hub for Black professionals and entrepreneurs in the early 20th century. Although based in the U.S., the principles of collective economic empowerment demonstrated by Black Wall Street can serve as inspiration for Black communities in the UK and Europe.

In the UK, **Brixton**, a historically Black neighbourhood in London, became a cultural and economic centre for Afro-Caribbean immigrants in the mid-20th century. Despite facing gentrification and systemic challenges, Brixton remains a symbol of Black resilience and economic empowerment in the UK.

6.2 Supporting Black-Owned Businesses

One of the most effective ways to build community wealth is by supporting Black-owned businesses. When Black professionals and consumers prioritise spending within their own communities, they help to create jobs, stimulate local economies, and circulate wealth.

6.2.1 The Importance of Buying Black

Supporting Black-owned businesses is a direct way to contribute to economic growth within Black communities. By purchasing goods and services from Black-owned enterprises, consumers can help businesses grow, reinvest in the community, and provide opportunities for future generations.

In the UK, initiatives like **Black Pound Day** encourage consumers to support Black-owned businesses on the first Saturday of each month. This movement has gained significant momentum and serves as a model for other European countries looking to increase support for Black entrepreneurs.

6.2.2 How to Find and Support Black-Owned Businesses

Finding and supporting Black-owned businesses is easier than ever, thanks to online directories and community networks. In the UK, platforms like **Black Rise, The Black Business Directory UK** and **Jamii** provide comprehensive listings of Black-owned businesses across various industries, from fashion and beauty to technology and consulting.

Across Europe, similar platforms are emerging to connect consumers with Black-owned businesses. Buy **Black Europe**, for instance, offers a directory of Black-owned businesses throughout the continent, enabling consumers to support entrepreneurs from France, Germany, the Netherlands, and beyond.

Action Steps:
- Make a commitment to regularly purchase from Black-owned businesses.
- Share information about Black-owned businesses on social media and within your networks.
- Attend events like the **UK Black Business Show** or similar initiatives in Europe to connect with Black entrepreneurs.

6.3 Investing in Local Communities

Investing in Black communities goes beyond supporting businesses. It also involves contributing to initiatives that address economic disparities, create opportunities for education and employment, and improve the overall quality of life for Black individuals. By reinvesting profits into local community projects, Black professionals and entrepreneurs can help build a sustainable economic infrastructure.

6.3.1 Community Investment Models

There are several ways Black professionals and entrepreneurs in the UK and Europe can invest in their local communities:

- **Community Land Trusts (CLTs):** CLTs are nonprofit organisations that acquire and hold land to benefit the community and ensure affordable housing. You can pool resources to create CLTs in neighbourhoods facing gentrification or displacement. This model helps preserve affordable housing and ensures that property ownership remains within the community.
- **Social Enterprises:** Social enterprises are businesses that prioritise social impact alongside profit. You can create social enterprises that address specific needs within their communities, such as youth employment, financial literacy, or housing access. In the UK, programs like **UnLtd** provide funding and support for social entrepreneurs focused on community development.
- **Crowdfunding and Cooperative Investment:** Cooperative investment models, such as community-owned businesses or investment funds, allow multiple people to pool resources to fund larger projects. This approach spreads financial risk and provides greater access to capital for Black-owned ventures.

6.3.2 Philanthropy and Giving Back

Giving back to the community is a critical aspect of wealth-building, as it ensures that future generations have the resources and opportunities needed to succeed. You can contribute to your communities through philanthropy, charitable donations, and mentorship programs.

- **Mentorship and Education:** Mentorship programs provide guidance, knowledge, and resources to young Black professionals and entrepreneurs. Initiatives like **The Aleto Foundation** in the UK and the **Africa-Europe Diaspora Development Platform (ADEPT)** in Europe offer mentorship and leadership development opportunities for Black youth.
- **Charitable Contributions:** Black philanthropists can support community organisations that provide education, housing, healthcare, and business support services. Donating to charities that serve Black communities ensures that essential services are available to those in need.

6.4 Cooperative Economics: Fostering Collective Wealth

Cooperative economics is the practice of pooling resources, sharing ownership, and making collective financial decisions for the benefit of a group or community. This approach has deep roots in African and Afro-Caribbean culture and can be a powerful tool for building community wealth.

6.4.1 Cooperative Business Models

Cooperative businesses are owned and controlled by their members, who share in the profits and decision-making processes. You can adopt cooperative business models to foster economic empowerment and collective wealth-building.

- **Worker Cooperatives:** In a worker cooperative, employees own and operate the business, sharing profits and decision-making responsibilities. Black professionals in industries such as healthcare, education, and retail can form worker cooperatives to ensure fair wages, job security, and shared financial benefits.
- **Consumer Cooperatives:** Consumer cooperatives are businesses owned by their customers. By creating cooperatives for essential services like food, banking, or healthcare, Black communities can keep wealth circulating within the group while meeting their everyday needs.

6.4.2 Credit Unions and Cooperative Lending

Credit unions are member-owned financial cooperatives that provide banking services, loans, and financial support to their members. For Black professionals and entrepreneurs, joining or creating a credit union can offer an alternative to traditional banking systems, which often discriminate against minority borrowers.

In the UK, organisations like **London Mutual Credit Union** provide accessible financial services to underserved communities, offering low-interest loans, savings accounts, and financial education programs. By supporting credit unions and cooperative lending institutions, Black individuals can gain better access to capital and support community wealth-building.

Community wealth-building is a vital component of generational wealth creation. By supporting Black-owned businesses, investing in local communities, and fostering cooperative economics, we can create sustainable economic ecosystems that empower future generations. Collective efforts strengthen the financial resilience of Black communities and ensure that wealth is not only accumulated but also shared and preserved.

Section 7: Legacy Building and Passing Wealth to Future Generations

Building wealth is only one part of the journey toward generational prosperity. The next critical step is ensuring that wealth is preserved and passed down effectively to future generations. This means creating a legacy that empowers their descendants to continue building upon the foundations of wealth.

In this section, we will explore the importance of financial literacy, estate planning, and family wealth strategies to prevent wealth erosion and ensure that assets are protected for future generations.

7.1 The Importance of Financial Literacy in Legacy Building

One of the most crucial aspects of passing down wealth is ensuring that future generations have the knowledge and skills to manage it effectively. Without proper financial literacy, wealth can easily be squandered or mismanaged, leaving subsequent generations without the same opportunities.

7.1.1 Teaching Financial Literacy to Children and Young Adults

For Black families, instilling financial literacy at an early age is essential for preserving and growing wealth across generations. Financial literacy involves understanding how to budget, save, invest, and manage credit, all of which are critical skills for wealth management.

- **Start Early:** Introducing children to basic financial concepts, such as saving and budgeting, at a young age sets the foundation for responsible financial behaviour. Parents can involve their children in family financial discussions, teaching them about money management in practical, everyday terms.
- **Programs and Resources:** There are many resources available to help teach financial literacy. In the UK, initiatives like **Young Money** and **The Financial Times' Financial Literacy and Inclusion Campaign** offer tools for teaching financial management skills to children and young adults. In Europe, similar programs such as Global Money Week encourage young people to learn about saving and investing.
- **Practical Lessons:** Encouraging teenagers and young adults to open savings accounts, manage small investments, or even start a side business can provide hands-on experience with money management. These practical lessons prepare them to handle larger sums responsibly in the future.

7.1.2 Family Wealth Education Programs

Establishing regular family meetings to discuss wealth-building strategies, estate planning, and financial goals can help ensure that every family member understands the importance of managing wealth. This practice also encourages transparency and accountability, preventing miscommunication or mismanagement of resources.

- **Example:** In many wealth-building families, parents or grandparents create family financial councils, where younger generations are taught about wealth management, business, and investing. These councils can foster a sense of responsibility and stewardship over family assets.

7.2 Estate Planning: Protecting and Transferring Wealth

Effective estate planning is a cornerstone of legacy building. Without proper planning, wealth can be eroded by taxes, legal disputes, or poor management. Estate planning ensures that assets are transferred smoothly to heirs while minimising taxes and protecting wealth for future generations.

7.2.1 Creating Wills and Trusts

Creating a will is essential for ensuring that assets are distributed according to their wishes. Without a will, the estate may go into probate, leading to delays, legal fees, and potentially unfavourable outcomes for heirs.

- **Wills:** A will outlines how assets should be distributed after death, ensuring that property, businesses, and investments are passed down to the intended beneficiaries. In the UK and many European countries, writing a will can also help minimise inheritance tax.
- **Trusts:** Trusts offer a more advanced form of estate planning, providing additional protections for wealth. Setting up a trust allows assets to be held and managed on behalf of beneficiaries. This can be particularly useful for controlling how and when wealth is distributed to heirs, especially younger or inexperienced family members.
- **Family Trusts:** Establishing family trusts can help protect family wealth from taxes, creditors, or mismanagement. Trusts can also ensure that wealth is used in accordance with specific wishes, such as funding education or supporting business ventures.

7.2.2 Minimising Inheritance Taxes

Inheritance taxes can significantly reduce the amount of wealth passed down to future generations. Proper tax planning is crucial for preserving wealth and ensuring that heirs receive the maximum benefit from their inheritance.

- **UK Inheritance Tax:** In the UK, inheritance tax can be up to **40%** on estates that exceed the threshold (currently £325,000). However, there are several ways to reduce this tax burden, such as gifting assets during one's lifetime, using trusts, and taking advantage of tax reliefs for business owners and agricultural land.
- **European Inheritance Laws:** In countries like France and Germany, inheritance taxes can vary depending on the relationship between the deceased and the heir. It's important to understand local inheritance laws and work with a tax advisor to create a plan that minimises tax liabilities.

7.2.3 Life Insurance as a Wealth Protection Tool

Life insurance is another essential tool for protecting wealth and ensuring that future generations are financially secure. By purchasing life insurance, Black professionals and entrepreneurs can provide their families with a financial safety net, covering expenses such as estate taxes, funeral costs, or debts.

- **Types of Life Insurance:** There are several types of life insurance policies available in the UK and Europe, including term life insurance (which provides coverage for a set period) and whole life insurance (which provides coverage for life). Whole life insurance policies often include an investment component, allowing families to grow wealth over time.

7.3 Building a Family Legacy Through Business and Property

Family-owned businesses and property are two of the most powerful tools for building and passing down wealth. By creating a family business or investing in real estate, Black professionals and entrepreneurs can ensure that future generations have assets that appreciate over time and generate income.

7.3.1 Family-Owned Businesses

A successful family-owned business can be passed down through generations, providing financial stability and a source of income for family members. In the UK and Europe, Black entrepreneurs have increasingly embraced family business models, which allow them to build wealth while involving future generations in business management.

- **Succession Planning:** Succession planning is critical for ensuring that the business continues to thrive after the founder retires or passes away. Clear succession plans outline who will take over the business, what training or education is required, and how ownership will be transferred.
- **Example:** A Black family running a successful real estate development firm in London might involve their children in the business from an early age, providing them with opportunities to learn the ropes. The founder can create a succession plan to ensure a smooth transition of leadership and ownership.

7.3.2 Real Estate Investments for Future Generations

Investing in real estate is a time-tested method for building wealth. Property appreciates over time and can generate rental income, providing financial security for future generations. By purchasing and maintaining income-generating properties, Black professionals can create a lasting legacy for their families.

- **Property Portfolios:** Building a diversified property portfolio—composed of residential, commercial, or even international properties—can provide multiple streams of income for future generations. In the UK, programs like **Buy-to-Let** enable individuals to purchase property and rent it out, generating consistent income.
- **Passing Down Property:** Real estate can be passed down to heirs, providing them with both a valuable asset and an ongoing income source. Estate planning tools such as trusts can help protect properties from excessive taxes and ensure that they remain within the family.

7.4 Avoiding Common Pitfalls in Wealth Transfer

Even with the best intentions, many families struggle to preserve wealth across generations. Common pitfalls such as lack of communication, mismanagement of assets, and poor financial literacy can result in wealth being diminished or lost entirely. To avoid these issues, Black professionals and entrepreneurs must take proactive steps to ensure that wealth is managed responsibly.

7.4.1 Open Family Discussions About Wealth

One of the most important steps in a successful wealth transfer is open communication within the family. Wealth-building families should engage in regular discussions about financial goals, estate plans, and the responsibilities that come with managing wealth. These conversations help ensure that every family member understands their role and the importance of preserving wealth for future generations.

7.4.2 Professional Management of Family Wealth

In some cases, it may be beneficial to enlist the help of professional wealth managers, accountants, or legal advisors to oversee family assets. These professionals can guide investment strategies, tax planning, and legal matters, helping to protect and grow the family's wealth over time.

Section 8: Inspiration from Black Wealth Builders

The journey to building generational wealth is challenging, but the success stories of Black professionals and entrepreneurs in the UK and Europe serve as powerful reminders that it is possible to overcome systemic barriers and create lasting financial legacies. By drawing inspiration from those who have paved the way, Black professionals can learn valuable lessons and gain motivation to pursue their own wealth-building journeys.

In this section, we will highlight several Black wealth builders in the UK and Europe, focusing on their challenges, strategies, and successes. These stories demonstrate the resilience, innovation, and determination needed to achieve long-term financial success.

8.1 Flavilla Fongang: A Multi-Award-Winning Entrepreneur and Global Leader

Flavilla Fongang is a dynamic, multi-award-winning serial entrepreneur and international keynote speaker. Her influence spans across multiple industries, including tech, branding, and education. Named by Computer Weekly as the most influential woman in tech in the UK in 2022, Fongang's journey is a testament to her expertise, resilience, and drive to create impactful change on a global scale. In 2023, she won The Entrepreneur of the Year Award at the BTA Awards and became a UN Women partner, furthering her commitment to supporting women's rights worldwide. She was also listed among the Global Top 100 Most Influential People of African Descent in 2024, alongside notable names like Will.i.am.

8.1.1 Challenges and Barriers

Flavilla Fongang's journey to success has been marked by her ability to navigate and overcome the systemic barriers that often confront Black women in business. Breaking into sectors such as tech and branding, where representation was limited, required persistence and strategic vision. Fongang had to establish credibility in a market where Black women were underrepresented, particularly in leadership positions. The challenges of overcoming societal expectations, balancing diverse ventures, and creating new paths where none existed did not deter her but fueled her passion for innovation and inclusivity.

8.1.2 Strategies for Success

Fongang's ventures span across branding, tech, and beyond, and her strategies for success have centred around innovation, diversity, and empowering others:

3 Colours Rule: Fongang founded this award-winning branding and marketing agency to help businesses harness the power of neuroscience-driven branding. Through her **D.A.C. system** and **Beyond Marketing Approach**, she has helped numerous brands grow by combining strategy, design, and customer experience.

GTA Black Women in Tech: Recognising the need for more representation of Black women in tech, Fongang created this platform, which has since become the largest European network for Black women professionals in the industry. With over 22,000 members, it has transformed into a space for collaboration, support, and the celebration of Black women in tech.

The Voices in The Shadow: Fongang's annual book highlights the stories of Black women in tech, inspiring future generations and promoting diversity in the industry. Distributed for free across schools in the UK and Ireland, the book has had a lasting impact, with over 2,200 copies given to schools and archived at The British Library to protect its legacy.

Creative Activism: In 2022, Fongang created an art collection addressing colourism and dark skin discrimination, showcasing the beauty and diversity of Black women. In 2023, she launched an interactive history map, highlighting the remarkable stories of Black women throughout history,

further cementing her commitment to using creative platforms for social change.

Global Influence: Her reach extends beyond the UK and Europe. Flavilla Fongang's ventures have reshaped the business landscape, using innovation, creativity, and strategic leadership to empower diverse communities. Whether it's through branding, tech, or creative activism, her contributions have helped pave the way for future generations of entrepreneurs and leaders.

8.2 Rob Pierre: Scaling Jellyfish into a Global Digital Powerhouse

Rob Pierre is the co-founder and former CEO of Jellyfish, a global digital marketing agency. Over 18 years, Pierre built Jellyfish from scratch into a global leader in digital marketing, driving annual revenues of $335 million. Pierre's leadership transformed Jellyfish into a trusted digital partner for world-renowned brands like Google, Netflix, and Uber. His journey highlights the determination, resilience, and innovative strategies required to thrive in a competitive industry while breaking barriers for underrepresented entrepreneurs.

8.2.1 Challenges and Barriers

Like many Black entrepreneurs, Pierre faced significant challenges in gaining initial visibility and credibility in the saturated digital marketing space. Establishing trust with high-profile clients was particularly challenging. Despite these hurdles, Pierre navigated the competitive environment by staying ahead of digital trends and relentlessly focusing on innovation and partnership.

One of the biggest turning points for Pierre was selling a majority stake in Jellyfish to French investment group Fimalac in 2019, in a deal that valued the company at £500 million. This partnership allowed Jellyfish to scale rapidly, employing over 2,000 people across 38 countries and expanding its client roster to include giants like Netflix and Google.

8.2.2 Strategies for Success

Pierre's strategy for success centred on investing in **technology and talent** while cultivating a unique company culture based on inclusivity, transparency, and innovation. One of his key innovations was developing a global training initiative during the pandemic, aimed at providing furloughed workers with valuable digital marketing skills—an initiative that garnered widespread recognition and helped Jellyfish strengthen its client relationships.

Another core element of Pierre's success was his **focus on diversity, equity, and inclusion (DEI)**. Under his leadership, Jellyfish became a company committed to ensuring representation and creating opportunities for people from underrepresented backgrounds, further differentiating the agency from its competitors.

Pierre's decision to step down from Jellyfish in 2023 followed an extended summer break after the company was sold to **Brandtech Group**. Reflecting on his 18-year journey, Pierre noted, "It's the right time for me to step away and focus on other ambitions, including projects that have the potential for wider societal impact." This sentiment reflects Pierre's ongoing commitment to making a difference beyond business—such as his involvement with the clothing brand **Inside Out**, co-founded in 2022, which creates opportunities for young ex-offenders in the fashion industry.

Pierre continues to be a shareholder in Jellyfish and his contributions to the industry were acknowledged when he was named **Media Leader of the Year** by Media Week in 2021, in recognition of his efforts in DEI, business achievements, and his innovative global training initiative during the pandemic. His business interests extend beyond Jellyfish, including ventures like **Infinity**, a call-tracking company, **Pro-Am Tour**, a golf business, and the **Mber** restaurant and bar in London.

Pierre's entrepreneurial journey underscores the importance of resilience, adaptability, and a relentless focus on building a business that fosters innovation, diversity, and long-term client success. His leadership has not only scaled Jellyfish to global heights but also left a lasting legacy of societal

8.3 Dr. Yvonne Thompson CBE: Advocacy and Leadership

Dr. Yvonne Thompson CBE is a British entrepreneur, author, and advocate for diversity in business. She is the founder of **Changing Faces**, a PR and communications agency, and has been a strong advocate for promoting diversity in corporate boardrooms. Thompson has served as a role model for countless Black professionals, demonstrating the importance of leadership, advocacy, and representation in achieving financial and professional success.

8.3.1 Challenges and Barriers

Thompson faced significant barriers in the early stages of her career, particularly as a Black woman in the communications industry. She encountered racial and gender discrimination, with many doubting her ability to succeed in a predominantly white, male-dominated field. Despite these challenges, she persisted and used her experiences to advocate for diversity in leadership.

8.3.2 Strategies for Success

Thompson's success stems from her dedication to promoting diversity and inclusion at the highest levels of business. She strategically positioned herself as a leader and expert in communications, while also advocating for greater representation of Black and minority professionals in corporate boardrooms.

Her work highlights the importance of advocacy and leadership in changing the narrative around diversity in business. Thompson's ability to balance entrepreneurship with social impact has made her a trailblazer in the UK's business community.

8.4 Mo Abudu: Media Mogul and Entrepreneur

Mo Abudu is a Nigerian-British media entrepreneur and the founder of **EbonyLife TV**, a leading African entertainment network. Based in Nigeria, Abudu's influence extends across Europe and the UK, where she has become a prominent figure in the media industry. Her success in creating and distributing African content on a global scale has inspired many Black entrepreneurs to pursue opportunities in media and entertainment.

8.4.1 Challenges and Barriers

Abudu faced significant challenges in establishing a media network that focused on African stories and perspectives. As a Black woman in the media industry, she encountered scepticism about the viability of her business model, especially when pitching to investors in a predominantly white industry.

8.4.2 Strategies for Success

Abudu's strategy was to create content that resonated with African and global audiences alike. She tapped into the growing demand for African stories in the media and positioned EbonyLife TV as a platform that celebrated African culture while addressing universal themes. By focusing on high-quality production and global distribution, Abudu was able to grow her brand and reach a global audience.

Her success illustrates the importance of identifying cultural trends, creating content that reflects diverse perspectives, and using media as a tool for empowerment and representation.

8.5 Alain Mabanckou: From Author to Entrepreneur

Alain Mabanckou is a Congolese-French writer, professor, and entrepreneur. His literary works have won numerous awards, and he has become a respected voice in both the literary and entrepreneurial worlds. Mabanckou's career demonstrates the intersection of creative talent and entrepreneurship, showing how Black individuals can turn their passions into profitable ventures.

8.5.1 Challenges and Barriers

Mabanckou faced the challenge of breaking into the French literary world, which has historically been dominated by white writers. As an African writer in Europe, he had to navigate the complexities of being an immigrant and a minority in a space that often marginalised Black voices.

8.5.2 Strategies for Success

Mabanckou's strategy was to remain authentic to his voice and heritage while building his career as a writer. He leveraged his unique perspective as an African writer living in France to create stories that resonated with a global audience. Beyond writing, Mabanckou expanded his career into academia and entrepreneurship, turning his literary success into a platform for social and cultural commentary. His story highlights the importance of persistence, cultural authenticity, and the ability to diversify one's talents in various fields. Mabanckou's career is a testament to how Black creatives can merge artistic expression with entrepreneurship to build lasting legacies.

8.6 Raphael Sofoluke: Creating Platforms for Black Professionals

Raphael Sofoluke is the founder of the **UK Black Business Show**, an annual event that brings together Black professionals, entrepreneurs, and business leaders from across the UK. The event, which showcases Black talent and provides networking opportunities, has become one of the largest platforms for celebrating and supporting Black entrepreneurship in the UK.

8.6.1 Challenges and Barriers

When Sofoluke launched the UK Black Business Show, he faced significant challenges in gaining visibility and support for his vision. In a business environment where Black entrepreneurs often struggle to access mainstream networks and funding, Sofoluke's mission was to create a space that celebrated Black business achievements and provided opportunities for networking and collaboration.

8.6.2 Strategies for Success

Sofoluke's strategy centred on identifying a gap in the market—Black professionals in the UK lacked a dedicated space to celebrate and promote their successes. By leveraging his network, building partnerships with sponsors, and using digital marketing to reach his target audience, Sofoluke grew the UK Black Business Show into a major event. His success demonstrates the importance of creating niche platforms that cater to underrepresented communities and the power of networking to build business visibility and influence.

The stories of Black wealth builders in the UK and Europe demonstrate that, despite systemic barriers, success is achievable through innovation, perseverance, and a strong sense of community. These individuals have paved the way for future generations by creating businesses, platforms, and opportunities that celebrate Black excellence and foster wealth-building. Their journeys remind us that wealth-building is not just about financial gain but also about creating legacies, advocating for change, and empowering others to follow in their footsteps. By learning from these examples, Black professionals and entrepreneurs can draw inspiration and find motivation to continue their own wealth-building journeys.

Flexible Task Plan for Building Generational Wealth

This task plan is designed to be adaptable, enabling you to focus on areas where you need the most growth while skipping or enhancing sections where you are already proficient. The tasks below are grouped into categories, and you can address them in any order that suits your current strengths and situation.

1. Awareness and Education: Laying the Foundation

Objective: Gain a deep understanding of the historical and systemic barriers to wealth-building in Black communities and equip yourself with the knowledge to overcome them.

Tasks:
- **Research historical challenges:** Study the racial wealth gap, housing discrimination, and systemic barriers specific to the Black community in the UK and Europe.
- **Understand the Economic Contributions of Black Communities:** Explore how Black communities, despite systemic barriers, have played a crucial role in the growth of the economy.
- **Enhance financial literacy:** Enroll in courses on economics, financial literacy, and wealth-building strategies (e.g., Coursera, LinkedIn Learning).
- **Attend community events:** Join forums or webinars to learn from experts about wealth inequality and actionable solutions for Black communities.
- **Outcome:** Build a solid foundation of knowledge that informs your wealth-building strategy. Document key learnings in a personal journal.

2. Strategic Action: Tailoring Your Wealth-Building Strategy

Objective: Develop a personalised wealth-building plan that aligns with your career, business goals, and financial situation.

Tasks:
- **Create a career/business growth plan:** Assess your current job or entrepreneurial opportunities. Identify certifications, career changes, or new business ideas to pursue.
- **Develop a savings and investment plan:** Use budgeting tools like Mint or YNAB to outline savings goals, and identify how much you can allocate toward investments.
- **Start a side business:** If entrepreneurship is part of your plan, develop a small-scale business that aligns with your skills and market demand.

Outcome: Have a wealth-building roadmap that outlines specific financial, entrepreneurial, and career milestones for the next 12 months.

3. Accessing Capital and Building Networks

Objective: Secure funding and build a robust network of mentors and peers to support your wealth-building efforts.
-

Tasks:
- **Identify and apply for funding:** Explore grants, loans, and venture capital specific to Black entrepreneurs (e.g., Black Business Fund, Colorintech).
- **Attend networking events:** Join professional groups and attend Black-led business events like the UK Black Business Show or Black Women in Tech.
- **Establish an emergency fund:** Begin saving 3-6 months' worth of living expenses to create financial security as you build your wealth.

Outcome: Secure funding for your business ventures or investments and establish a strong network of business connections.

4. Investment and Asset Building: Growing Your Wealth

Objective: Start building and diversifying your investment portfolio, including real estate, stocks, and business ownership.

Tasks:
- **Start investing:** Use platforms like Hargreaves Lansdown or Trading 212 to invest in UK and European stocks, ETFs, or bonds.
- **Explore real estate:** Attend property investment seminars and research government programs (Help to Buy, Shared Ownership) to purchase your first property.
- **Expand your side business:** If you've started a business, focus on scaling it to generate additional income.

Outcome: Create a diversified portfolio, including stocks, real estate, and a business, that grows your wealth over time.

5. Family Legacy Planning: Protecting and Passing Down Wealth

Objective: Ensure that your wealth is preserved and transferred to future generations through estate planning and family financial education.

Tasks:
- **Draft a will and trust:** Work with a solicitor or estate planner to create a will and set up a family trust to protect assets.
- **Educate your family:** Teach family members about wealth management, budgeting, and investments to prepare them for handling inherited wealth.
- **Plan for inheritance taxes:** Understand UK and European inheritance laws and work with a financial planner to minimise tax liabilities.

Outcome: Establish legal structures to ensure your wealth is protected and passed down smoothly, and that future generations are financially literate.

6. Community Wealth-Building: Strengthening Collective Wealth

Objective: Contribute to community wealth by supporting Black-owned businesses and investing in local development.

Tasks:
- **Support Black-owned businesses:** Commit to buying from Black-owned businesses regularly and share their information within your networks.
- **Invest in community projects:** Contribute to crowdfunding or cooperative models that promote community wealth (e.g., Community Land Trusts).
- **Mentor others:** Offer mentorship to aspiring Black entrepreneurs or students to help them navigate the wealth-building process.

Outcome: Foster collective economic growth by supporting your community and mentoring future generations.

7. Consistency, Patience, and Adaptation: Maintaining Momentum

Objective: Stay consistent with your wealth-building efforts, adapt strategies as needed, and remain committed to long-term success.

Tasks:
- **Regular financial reviews:** Schedule quarterly reviews to assess your investment portfolio and wealth-building progress.
- **Continue learning:** Take at least one new course annually on advanced investing,

entrepreneurship, or wealth management.
- **Mentor and give back:** Consistently offer mentorship or advice to others in your community as a way of paying forward your success.

Outcome: Maintain steady wealth accumulation while ensuring you continue to adapt your strategies to evolving financial landscapes.

How to Customise the Plan Based on Your Strengths

1. **Focus on Your Weakest Areas:**
Prioritise sections where you need the most growth. For instance, if you're strong in investment but need better community involvement, start with Community Wealth-Building.

2. **Skip What You've Mastered:**
If you're already advanced in financial literacy or estate planning, you can jump to more complex tasks like expanding your investment portfolio or mentoring others.

3. **Parallel Progress:**
You can work on investment and building networks simultaneously. For example, while growing your stock portfolio, you can attend networking events to connect with investors or mentors.

Measurable Milestones and Key Performance Indicators (KPIs)

- **Month 1:** Complete awareness and education phase, building a strong foundation of knowledge about wealth inequality and wealth-building strategies.
- **Month 3:** Create a wealth-building strategy and secure at least one funding source.
- **Month 6:** Begin investments in the stock market, real estate, or a business, with at least one asset acquired or investment made.
- **Month 9:** Complete family legacy planning, including drafting a will and educating family members on financial management.
- **Month 12:** Actively support Black-owned businesses and participate in community investments, with measurable contributions.

This task plan allows you to tackle the various components of wealth-building in a flexible, customised way. Whether you're just starting out or already well-versed in specific areas, this roadmap gives you the tools to focus on your specific needs, making progress at your own pace. The ultimate goal is to not only build wealth for yourself but to foster community growth and ensure your legacy endures across generations.

By following this adaptable approach, you are positioning yourself to succeed in the journey toward **generational wealth**—creating not only financial security but also empowering those around you to rise together.

Conclusion of this guide: Moving Forward with Purpose

As we conclude this guide, the overarching message is clear: building generational wealth is possible, even in the face of systemic challenges. By following the wealth-building framework laid out in this book—awareness, strategic action, accessing resources, investment, financial planning, community wealth-building, and legacy preservation—Black professionals and entrepreneurs in the UK and Europe can take actionable steps toward creating lasting financial legacies.

Whether through entrepreneurship, investment, education, or community efforts, the path to generational wealth requires persistence, resilience, and a commitment to empowering future generations. As more Black individuals take control of their financial futures, they will not only close the racial wealth gap but also contribute to a broader movement of economic empowerment for Black communities across the UK and Europe.

Moving Forward with Purpose and Black Rise

The journey to building generational wealth as a Black professional or entrepreneur in the UK and Europe is complex, often requiring us to navigate systemic challenges and overcome barriers that have been in place for centuries. Yet, as we've explored throughout this book, the path to wealth-building is achievable through strategic action, education, investment, and community collaboration.

At the heart of this journey is the understanding that **we do not rise alone—we rise together**. And this is where **Black Rise** plays a critical role. Black Rise serves as the platform where **Black talent connects** with opportunities to drive business success and accelerate careers. It exists to ensure that Black professionals and entrepreneurs are not only building individual wealth but also contributing to the collective progress of the community.

Why Black Rise Matters

In a world where access to networks, mentorship, and resources is often unequally distributed, Black Rise steps in as a powerful connector. The platform fosters collaboration, growth, and visibility for Black professionals and entrepreneurs, helping them achieve their business goals by harnessing the power of Black talent, data insights, and business solutions.

Black Rise provides the infrastructure for success in three critical ways:

1. **Connecting Black Talent:** Through a global network of Black professionals, entrepreneurs, and businesses, Black Rise facilitates access to opportunities, including partnerships, collaborations, and investment. This ensures that Black talent is seen, heard, and given the tools needed to thrive in competitive industries.
2. **Driving Business Success:** Black Rise is focused on supporting Black entrepreneurs and professionals by facilitating access to business opportunities. Whether it's showcasing Black talent to institutions or building credibility in the business world, Black Rise ensures that the profiles of Black entrepreneurs and professionals are elevated to their rightful place on the global stage.
3. **Empowering Collective Progress:** The platform encourages a collective approach to economic empowerment. By uniting Black professionals with Black-focused organisations, enterprises, and investors, Black Rise creates an ecosystem where Black talent not only succeeds individually but also contributes to the larger goal of economic equity.

Where Black Talent Connects to Drive Success

Through **video-driven content** featuring **Black voices**, the platform provides learning resources, mentorship opportunities, and real-life examples of how Black professionals and entrepreneurs are succeeding in their fields. This kind of visibility is crucial for ensuring that Black talent is not only acknowledged but celebrated and nurtured.

What makes Black Rise unique is its focus on **showcasing Black talent** for institutions, building credibility and access for individuals, and facilitating career and business growth through a data-driven approach. It recognises that Black professionals are not limited by their potential but by the barriers they face, and it actively works to dismantle those barriers by connecting individuals to the right resources and networks.

We Rise Together

As we conclude this book, the message remains clear: **Black Rise** is not just a platform; it is a movement. It is a call to action for Black professionals and entrepreneurs to take control of their financial futures, to collaborate, and to collectively pursue economic equity. It's about fostering connections, creating opportunities, and driving growth that benefits not just individuals but entire communities.

Black Rise understands that when one of us rises, we all rise. That is why it is open to all, with a focus on supporting the Black community towards **equity** and **collective progress**. This mission aligns perfectly with the broader theme of this book: building generational wealth is not only possible, but it is essential for achieving long-term prosperity and closing the racial wealth gap.

As Black professionals and entrepreneurs across the UK, Europe, and beyond engage with platforms like Black Rise, they tap into a powerful network designed to uplift, empower, and ensure that **Black excellence** translates into **Black prosperity**.

Final Thoughts:

The pursuit of wealth-building is not an isolated journey. Through strategic investment, financial literacy, community building, and legacy planning, Black professionals and entrepreneurs can create generational wealth that secures their future and the future of their families. **Black Rise** *is the platform that helps you make that vision a reality—by providing the connections, resources, and opportunities to rise together, we drive progress for all.*

Next, you'll dive into **59 business chess moves**—*fictional stories crafted to help you understand the strategies needed to thrive as a Black professional or entrepreneur. Though the stories aren't real, the* **wisdom** *in them is. They're designed to equip you with the insight and tactics necessary to overcome challenges, make bold moves, and achieve your goals.*

As you embark on your wealth-building journey, remember that you are part of a larger movement towards economic equity. Through Black Rise and the lessons from this book, you have the tools to not only build wealth but also to inspire, uplift, and support others in their rise to success.

Together, we are stronger. Together, **we rise.**

Flavilla Fongang

01. The Power of Empathy and Continuous Learning in Leadership

In the business world, especially in leadership, empathy and continuous learning are not just soft skills—they are strategic imperatives. Leaders who actively listen, show empathy, and commit to lifelong learning are more effective in guiding their teams, driving innovation, and overcoming challenges.

In the bustling city of Atlanta, Kwame Adeyemi, a rising star in the tech industry, was known for his sharp intellect and relentless work ethic. However, as he ascended the corporate ladder, Kwame realised that technical expertise alone wasn't enough to lead effectively. One pivotal moment came during a high-stakes project that required collaboration across multiple departments, each with its own set of challenges and expectations.

Among his team were Aisha Thompson, a skilled project manager with a knack for bringing out the best in her colleagues, and Jelani Mbemba, a creative genius from the marketing team with roots in the Caribbean. Despite their talents, the project faced delays, and tensions were running high.

Kwame, driven by a desire to succeed, initially focused on the technical aspects of the project, pushing his team hard to meet deadlines. However, he soon noticed that morale was dipping, and the innovative spark that Jelani usually brought to the table was dimming. Aisha, usually a beacon of positivity, seemed increasingly withdrawn.

Realising that something was amiss, Kwame decided to take a step back and reflect on his approach. He remembered advice from his mentor, an experienced leader named Nkechi Okafor, who had always emphasised the importance of empathy and continuous learning in leadership. "Kwame," she had once said, "Leadership isn't just about getting things done; it's about how you get things done, and that means understanding the people who are helping you achieve those goals."

Taking this to heart, Kwame called a team meeting—not to discuss project timelines, but to listen. He invited Aisha and Jelani to share their thoughts, concerns, and ideas in an open and supportive environment. To his surprise, Aisha revealed that she felt overwhelmed by the workload and unsure about how to balance the competing demands. Jelani admitted that the pressure to deliver was stifling his creativity, making it difficult for him to innovate.

Kwame realised that he had been so focused on the end goal that he had neglected the well-being and input of his team. Determined to turn things around, he decided to make empathy and continuous learning the cornerstones of his leadership approach.

He started by actively listening to his team members, ensuring they felt heard and valued. He practised empathy by considering their perspectives and challenges, making adjustments to the project plan that allowed for more flexibility and creativity. Kwame also committed to continuous learning, seeking out leadership courses and engaging in mentorship with Nkechi to improve his skills.

The results were transformative. Aisha, feeling more supported, was able to manage the project more effectively, while Jelani, with the space to breathe, brought forth a groundbreaking marketing strategy that propelled the project to success. The team not only met their deadlines but also exceeded expectations, delivering a product that was innovative and well-received by the market.

Kwame's journey is a testament to the power of empathy and continuous learning in leadership. By listening to his team, practising empathy, and embracing personal growth, he was able to turn a struggling project into a success and, in the process, became a more effective and respected leader.

The worst thing that you can do to yourself is not take those chances to learn and to grow. If you fail, at least you learn something.

Key Action Points from Kwame's Story

- **Listen Actively:** Like Kwame, make it a habit to truly listen to your team. Understand their challenges, concerns, and aspirations to build trust and foster collaboration.
- **Practice Empathy:** Put yourself in others' shoes, as Kwame did. Empathy can break down barriers and create a supportive work environment.
- **Embrace Continuous Learning:** Kwame's commitment to learning from his experiences and seeking mentorship highlights the importance of staying adaptable and open to new ideas.
- **Challenge Yourself and Others:** Growth often happens at the edge of discomfort. Kwame's willingness to challenge himself and his team led to innovation and success.

02. Building Resilience, Strategies for Entrepreneurial Success

When launching a business, the urge to present a polished, professional image from the start can lead to excessive spending and financial strain. A more sustainable approach is to start lean, focusing on essential expenditures, while remaining adaptable and resilient through challenges.

Makena Kinyua, a young and ambitious entrepreneur from Kenya, stared at the blank walls of her modest workspace in Nairobi. It wasn't the sleek, modern office she had once dreamed of, but it was the beginning of something meaningful. Makena had just launched her tech startup, an innovative platform aimed at connecting smallholder farmers in East Africa with vital resources like seeds, fertilisers, and market access.

Makena knew that her vision had the potential to transform lives across the region, but she also understood the challenges ahead. Many startups in Nairobi's fast-growing tech scene had burned through their funds quickly, prioritising appearances over sustainable growth. Makena was determined not to fall into that trap.

Instead of renting an expensive office in one of Nairobi's upscale business districts, Makena chose a small, affordable co-working space in a less glamorous part of the city. The space was shared with other startups, which not only kept costs low but also fostered a sense of community and collaboration. Makena invested her limited funds where it mattered most—hiring a small but skilled team of developers, conducting thorough market research, and refining her platform's user experience.

In the early days, Makena and her team faced numerous challenges. There were times when cash flow was tight, and the temptation to secure a loan to "impress" potential investors with a more polished image was strong. But Makena remained focused on her long-term vision. She understood that every shilling spent on non-essential items was a shilling less for product development and customer acquisition.

Her frugality and strategic thinking paid off when the platform began to gain traction. Word spread quickly among the farming communities, and soon, Makena's startup was recognised for its impact and potential. Investors started to take notice—not because of a flashy office or an impressive facade, but because of the platform's tangible success and the clear demand for its services.

Makena's ability to stay lean and adaptable also allowed her to pivot quickly when needed. When data revealed that farmers needed more support with logistics and distribution, Makena quickly reallocated resources to develop this aspect of the platform, ensuring that it met the real needs of her users.

As her startup grew, Makena continued to prioritise essential investments. She focused on scaling operations and expanding the platform's reach across East Africa, always guided by the principle of financial prudence and strategic growth.

Start to think about people who are actually doing this already and see how far that investment can go. We need to be intentional.

Key Action Points from Makena's Story

- **Start Lean and Focus on Essentials:** Like Makena, prioritise spending on areas that directly contribute to your business's core operations and growth. Avoid unnecessary expenses in the early stages, such as high-end office spaces or large teams, until your business can sustain them.
- **Remain Flexible and Adaptable:** Be prepared to make quick, strategic decisions when challenges arise. Makena's willingness to pivot and reallocate resources based on user needs helped her maintain financial health and ensure the platform's success.
- **Invest Where It Counts:** Direct your investments towards areas that will generate tangible returns. For Makena, this meant focusing on product development and customer acquisition rather than appearances.
- **Leverage Community Resources:** Sharing resources, such as co-working spaces, can keep costs low while fostering a collaborative environment. Makena's choice to work in a communal space helped her conserve funds while building valuable connections.

03. The Power of Building Advocacy and Sponsorship for Career Growth

To succeed in your career, especially in challenging environments, it's essential to build strong advocacy and sponsorship networks. These networks go beyond mere mentorship; they involve creating relationships with individuals who will actively support your growth and help open doors to new opportunities.

Nia Biko, a talented professional from Cameroon, had always been passionate about technology and innovation. After earning her degree in computer science, Nia secured a position at a leading tech firm in Silicon Valley. As one of the few African professionals in her company, she was determined to excel—not just for herself, but also to create a path for others like her.

Nia's technical skills were exceptional. She quickly gained a reputation for solving complex problems and delivering projects that exceeded expectations. However, despite her consistent performance, Nia noticed that her career progression wasn't aligning with her contributions. She realised that technical expertise alone wasn't enough; she needed to build a network of advocates and sponsors who could help elevate her career.

One day, Nia presented her innovative ideas for a new software platform at a company-wide innovation summit. In the audience was Michael Chen, a senior executive known for his influence and dedication to developing talent within the company. Impressed by Nia's presentation, Michael approached her afterward to discuss her vision in more detail.

Recognising the potential of this connection, Nia made a deliberate effort to cultivate a relationship with Michael. She sought his feedback on her projects, shared her career goals, and asked for advice on navigating the complexities of the tech industry. Michael appreciated Nia's proactive approach and was impressed by her consistent delivery of high-quality work.

Over time, Michael became more than just a mentor—he became an advocate for Nia. He spoke highly of her in executive meetings, highlighting her innovative ideas and her potential as a future leader within the company. Michael's support helped Nia gain visibility at the highest levels of the organisation, and soon, she was being considered for roles that had previously seemed out of reach.

However, Nia understood that advocacy alone wouldn't be enough. She needed a sponsor—someone with the influence to open doors and propel her career forward. During one of her conversations with Michael, Nia expressed her interest in leading a new international project the company was launching in Africa. Michael recognised the value Nia could bring to the project and decided to sponsor her for the position.

With Michael's sponsorship, Nia was selected to lead the project—a significant milestone in her career. The project's success not only established Nia as a leader within the company but also positioned her as an influential figure in the tech industry's African market.

Nia's journey from a skilled engineer to a recognised leader illustrates the power of building advocacy and sponsorship networks. By identifying and cultivating relationships with individuals who could advocate for her work and sponsor her career growth, Nia was able to navigate the challenges of her environment and achieve her career goals.

If you do good work with people, you build a rapport and you grow a network that know what you're capable of.

Key Action Points from Nia's Story

- **Identify Potential:** Advocates and Sponsors: Like Nia, seek out influential individuals within your organisation who recognise your work and can advocate for you in key discussions.
- **Communicate Your Vision:** Nia's success was partly due to her ability to clearly articulate her career goals and vision to Michael. Make sure your potential advocates and sponsors understand your aspirations.
- **Deliver Consistently:** Nia's consistent delivery of high-quality work earned her the respect and support of her advocate, Michael. Build your reputation through excellence.
- **Engage in Honest Conversations:** Regularly share your progress with your sponsors and advocates, as Nia did with Michael. This helps maintain strong relationships and keeps them invested in your growth.

04. The Power of Strategic Networking and Value Creation

Strategic networking and understanding your unique value proposition are crucial elements for long-term success and impact in business. Building authentic relationships, leveraging opportunities, and understanding how to add value to others can open doors that might otherwise remain closed

Jabari Mensah, a dynamic professional from Ghana, stood on the balcony of his small office in the heart of Cape Town, South Africa. The vibrant city buzzed below him, a mix of cultures, languages, and endless possibilities. Jabari had moved to Cape Town three years ago with nothing but a vision and an unwavering belief in the power of strategic networking and value creation.

Jabari had always been a natural networker. Even back in Accra, where he was raised, he had a knack for connecting with people from all walks of life. But Cape Town was different—more competitive, more diverse, and full of challenges that would test his limits. He knew that to succeed here, he had to not only work hard but also work smart.

His breakthrough came when he met Sarah Thompson, a seasoned entrepreneur and investor, at a local business conference. Sarah, who was originally from London but had made Cape Town her home, was impressed by Jabari's vision of creating a sustainable fashion brand that celebrated African heritage while empowering local artisans. However, it wasn't just his idea that caught her attention; it was the way Jabari understood the value he brought to the table—his deep connections with artisans across Ghana, his knowledge of sustainable practices, and his passion for African culture.

Instead of immediately pitching his business for investment, Jabari focused on building a relationship with Sarah. He took the time to understand her business interests, her vision for the future, and the challenges she faced. Over several months, Jabari and Sarah exchanged ideas, collaborated on small projects, and even co-hosted a workshop on sustainable business practices in Cape Town. Through this collaboration, Jabari not only gained Sarah's trust but also access to her extensive network of investors, business leaders, and influencers

One evening, during a dinner with some of these new connections, an opportunity arose that would change Jabari's life. A major retail chain was looking to partner with a sustainable brand to launch a new line of products. The project was high-profile and risky, but it was exactly the kind of challenge Jabari had been preparing for. With Sarah's endorsement and his own network of African artisans, Jabari secured the deal.

The partnership was a resounding success, catapulting Jabari's brand into the spotlight and opening doors across the continent. His business grew, and so did his influence. But Jabari never forgot the lessons he had learned: the importance of strategic networking, the value of authentic relationships, and the power of understanding and articulating his unique value.

Jabari's journey in Cape Town became a testament to the idea that success in business is about more than just hard work or a great idea. It's about strategically positioning yourself in the right networks, offering value to others before seeking anything in return, and being ready to seize opportunities when they arise.

As Jabari stood on his balcony, overlooking the city that had become his new home, he reflected on the quote that had guided him through his journey: "I'm not looking at a 50-year horizon for there to be equity in this world. I'm looking for a five-year horizon." He smiled, knowing that with the right network and a clear understanding of his value, anything was possible.

I'm not looking at a 50-year horizon for there to be equity in this world. I'm looking for a 5-year horizon.

Key Action Points from Jabari's Story

- **Focus on Building Relationships First:** Jabari's initial approach with Sarah Thompson highlights the importance of prioritising relationship-building over immediate pitches for investment.
- **Leverage Existing Networks for Growth:** Jabari's ability to access Sarah's network of investors, business leaders, and influencers was crucial in advancing his business.
- **Prepare for and Seize Opportunities:** Jabari was ready to capitalise on a major opportunity when the retail chain partnership emerged. His preparation and readiness to tackle high-profile projects were key to his success.
- **Articulate and Utilise Your Unique Value:** Jabari's success was partly due to his ability to clearly articulate and leverage his unique value proposition, which included his connections with African artisans, knowledge of sustainable practices, and passion for African culture.

05. The Power of Resilience and Strategic Focus in Entrepreneurship

Resilience and strategic focus are essential components for achieving long-term success in business. Challenges are inevitable, but how you respond to them can determine your trajectory. By maintaining a strong support system, continuously learning, and strategically navigating obstacles, you can turn setbacks into stepping stones toward greater

Zara Mensah, a determined entrepreneur from Ghana, had always been passionate about creating sustainable fashion that celebrated African heritage. She founded ZM Couture, a fashion brand based in Accra, focused on producing high-quality, ethically made clothing using traditional African textiles. Zara's vision was to not only build a successful brand but also to empower local artisans and promote African culture on the global stage.

However, Zara's journey was far from smooth. Early on, ZM Couture faced significant challenges, including supply chain disruptions, stiff competition, and financial constraints. Despite having a strong brand concept, Zara struggled to scale her business. She quickly realised that passion alone wasn't enough to overcome the obstacles in her path—she needed a more strategic approach and a resilient mindset.

One of the turning points for Zara was when she decided to seek mentorship from experienced entrepreneurs in the fashion industry. She reached out to a successful Ghanaian designer who had made a name internationally, and through this connection, she gained invaluable insights into scaling her business. Her mentor emphasised the importance of building a robust support system and diversifying her revenue streams to protect her business from unforeseen disruptions.

Zara took this advice to heart. She started by building stronger relationships with her suppliers, ensuring she had multiple sources for her materials to avoid dependency on a single supplier. She also expanded ZM Couture's product line to include accessories and home decor items, allowing her to tap into new markets and diversify her income.

In addition to these strategic moves, Zara leaned heavily on her personal support system—her family and close friends—who provided emotional support during the tough times. This network helped her stay focused and resilient, even when the business hit rough patches.

Another critical lesson Zara learned was the power of leveraging feedback. When sales stagnated, she didn't just push harder on the same strategies. Instead, she actively sought feedback from her customers and used it to refine her designs and marketing approach. This willingness to adapt based on feedback allowed Zara to better align her brand with market demands, ultimately leading to a significant uptick in sales.

Zara's resilience and strategic focus paid off. ZM Couture grew from a small local business to a brand with international recognition, showcasing at fashion weeks in London and Paris.

Her story became a testament to the power of resilience, strategic focus, and the importance of building a strong support system in the journey of entrepreneurship.

Challenges are inevitable, but how you respond to them can turn setbacks into stepping stones for greater achievements.

Key Action Points from Zara's Story

- **Build a Strong Support System:** Like Zara, surround yourself with people who believe in your vision and can provide both emotional and strategic support. A robust support system can help you navigate the challenges of entrepreneurship more effectively.
- **Leverage Feedback:** Use feedback from customers and mentors to refine your business strategy. Zara's ability to adapt based on feedback was crucial in aligning her brand with market demands.
- **Don't Put All Your Eggs in One Basket:** Diversify your client base and revenue streams. Zara expanded her product line and built multiple supplier relationships to protect her business from unforeseen disruptions.
- **Say Yes to Opportunities:** Even if you're unsure how to execute them fully at the moment, take on new opportunities and figure out the details as you go. Zara's proactive approach opened doors to international markets.

06. Navigating Change and Seizing Opportunities in a Career Path

Regular self-reflection is crucial for career growth and satisfaction. By consistently evaluating your career trajectory and the enjoyment you derive from your work, you can make informed decisions about when to pivot, seek new opportunities, or double down on your current path.

Yasmina El-Khoury, a talented marketing executive from Morocco, had always been driven by a passion for creativity and innovation. After completing her education in Paris, Yasmina returned to Casablanca, where she quickly climbed the ranks in a leading multinational company. Her role as a brand manager allowed her to work on high-profile campaigns and collaborate with some of the brightest minds in the industry. However, after several years of rapid career advancement, Yasmina began to feel a sense of restlessness.

Yasmina was aware that career satisfaction isn't static; it evolves over time. She had always been diligent about setting goals and achieving them, but now she felt a growing disconnect between her day-to-day work and her long-term aspirations. To address this, Yasmina decided to incorporate regular self-reflection into her routine. Twice a year, she set aside time to evaluate her career trajectory, assess her level of enjoyment, and consider whether her current role still aligned with her goals.

During one of these reflection points, Yasmina realised that while she still loved marketing, the excitement she once felt was waning. She recognized that her restlessness was not just temporary boredom but a deeper need for a new challenge. However, rather than making an impulsive decision, Yasmina took a strategic approach. She explored whether there were opportunities within her current company that could reignite her passion.

After discussions with her manager, she was offered a new role that involved leading a regional expansion project—an opportunity that allowed her to blend her love for marketing with her interest in international business.

Yasmina embraced the new role with enthusiasm, and it rekindled her excitement for her career. However, she remained committed to her practice of self-reflection. She continued to assess her satisfaction levels, ensuring that her career choices were aligned with her evolving goals.

Beyond her professional achievements, Yasmina also focused on building strong relationships within her industry. She invested time in networking and nurturing connections with colleagues, clients, and industry peers. These relationships not only enriched her career but also opened doors to unexpected opportunities, such as speaking engagements and consulting projects.

Eventually, another reflection point led Yasmina to a pivotal decision. She realised that while she was thriving in her role, she had a growing desire to start her own business—a marketing consultancy that would allow her to work with diverse clients across the Middle East and North Africa. Armed with the confidence that came from years of self-reflection and strategic decision-making, Yasmina made the bold move to leave her corporate role and launch her consultancy.

Her decision proved to be the right one. Yasmina's consultancy quickly gained traction, and she found immense satisfaction in building her own brand and helping other businesses succeed.

Having a reflection point for yourself at various points in the year is crucial - what am I getting out of my current role, my current job, and am I enjoying it?

Key Action Points from Yasmina's Story

- **Set Regular Reflection Points:** Like Yasmina, allocate specific times during the year to assess your career. Ask yourself if you still enjoy your work, if it aligns with your future goals, and if you feel excited about your daily tasks.
- **Differentiate Between Boredom and Burnout:** Recognise when you're just in need of a new challenge within your current role versus when it's time to explore new opportunities elsewhere. Yasmina's self-reflection helped her identify when it was time for a change.
- **Focus on Building Relationships:** Beyond technical skills, invest in relationships with colleagues, clients, and industry peers. This not only enriches your career but can also open doors to unexpected opportunities, as it did for Yasmina.
- **Be Prepared to Pivot:** If your reflection reveals dissatisfaction, don't be afraid to explore new roles, industries, or even geographical locations. Yasmina's decision to start her own consultancy was the result of thoughtful self-reflection and a willingness to pivot.

07. The Power of Strategic Collaboration for Growth in Business

Collaboration is more than just working with others; it's about aligning visions and creating value for all parties involved. In business, strategic collaboration can lead to exponential growth, innovation, and the realisation of shared goals.

Osei Badu, a visionary entrepreneur originally from Ghana, had always been passionate about sustainable technology. After completing his studies in environmental engineering, Osei moved to Lisbon, Portugal, to explore opportunities in Europe's growing green technology sector. Lisbon's vibrant and diverse entrepreneurial scene was the perfect environment for Osei to bring his innovative ideas to life, but he quickly realised that to truly make an impact, he needed to collaborate strategically with others who shared his vision. Osei's company, EcoWave Solutions, focused on developing sustainable energy solutions tailored to coastal communities.

However, as a newcomer to the Lisbon market, he faced challenges in scaling his business and gaining the traction needed to compete with established players. Osei understood that to achieve his ambitious goals, he would need to collaborate with others who could complement his strengths and help him realise his vision.

Osei began by identifying potential partners whose goals and vision aligned with his own. He connected with Sofia Mendes, a Portuguese entrepreneur who had successfully launched several environmental initiatives across Europe. Sofia was known for her deep understanding of the European market and her ability to bring together diverse stakeholders to drive impactful projects. Recognizing the alignment in their goals, Osei reached out to Sofia, proposing a collaboration that could combine EcoWave's innovative technology with Sofia's market expertise and extensive network.

Sofia, impressed by Osei's knowledge and passion, agreed to the partnership. Together, they crafted a strategy that not only leveraged their individual strengths but also created value for both their companies. Sofia's market insights helped Osei navigate regulatory challenges and connect with potential investors, while Osei's technical expertise brought a new dimension to Sofia's projects, enabling them to offer cutting-edge solutions to their clients.

Through their collaboration, Osei and Sofia were able to secure significant funding and expand EcoWave's operations across several European markets. The partnership was a win-win situation: Osei gained access to resources and networks that accelerated his company's growth, while Sofia's business benefited from the innovative technologies that set them apart from the competition.

Osei also stayed open to learning throughout the collaboration. He absorbed valuable lessons from Sofia's experience in the European market, which allowed him to refine his approach and better position EcoWave for success. This openness to different perspectives led to innovative solutions that neither of them could have developed alone. The collaboration between Osei and Sofia not only led to business growth but also contributed to the broader goal of promoting sustainable energy solutions across Europe. Their aligned visions and complementary strengths created a partnership that was greater than the sum of its parts, demonstrating the power of strategic collaboration in achieving shared goals.

If you collaborate with other individuals it's about getting someone on board, aligning visions, and creating magic together.

Key Action Points from Osei's Story

- **Identify Alignment:** Like Osei, before entering a partnership or collaboration, ensure that your goals and vision align with those of your potential partners. This alignment is crucial for long-term success.
- **Lead with Knowledge:** Always bring expertise to the table. Osei's deep knowledge of sustainable technology increased his credibility and influence in his collaboration with Sofia.
- **Create Value for All:** Aim to create win-win situations in your collaborations. Osei and Sofia's partnership was successful because it provided valuable outcomes for both parties involved.
- **Stay Open to Learning:** Be willing to learn from those you collaborate with, especially if they bring different perspectives or experiences to the table. Osei's openness to learning from Sofia's market expertise led to innovative solutions and new opportunities.

08. The Power of Networking and Human Connection in Business Success

In business, your network and the strength of your relationships are as crucial as your skills and knowledge. Building and nurturing connections can open doors to opportunities that might otherwise remain inaccessible, especially for those from underrepresented backgrounds.

Yanella Ndong, a determined entrepreneur from Cameroon, had always been passionate about the intersection of culture and fashion. After studying fashion design in Douala, she moved to Paris, the heart of the global fashion industry, with the dream of launching her own fashion label that celebrated African heritage while appealing to a global audience.

However, Yanella quickly discovered that breaking into the highly competitive Parisian fashion scene required more than just talent—it demanded strong networks and influential connections.

Despite her creative brilliance, Yanella struggled to gain traction. She found it difficult to secure funding, access prestigious fashion events, and connect with industry insiders who could help elevate her brand. These challenges were compounded by the fact that she was relatively new to Paris and had few connections in the industry.

Recognising the importance of building a strong network, Yanella began to actively seek out opportunities to meet people who could help her navigate the Paris fashion world. She attended industry events, joined fashion and cultural groups, and reached out to established designers and entrepreneurs for advice.

One such connection was with Sophie Dubois, a well-respected French fashion editor. Sophie saw the potential in Yanella's unique designs and offered to mentor her, guiding her on how to position her brand in the competitive market. With Sophie's mentorship, Yanella learned to navigate the complexities of the fashion industry in Paris. She was introduced to key players, gained insights into the industry's "rules of engagement," and slowly began to build her reputation. Through these connections, Yanella secured a spot in a prestigious Paris fashion show, which became the turning point for her brand.

Yanella's persistence in building and leveraging her network paid off. Her fashion line, which blended contemporary styles with traditional Cameroonian textiles, was met with critical acclaim. Her brand began to gain recognition, not just in Paris but internationally. The relationships she had cultivated helped her secure investment, media coverage, and partnerships that propelled her business forward.

Build relationships that are rooted in trust, shared values, and mutual respect, and they will be the foundation of your success.

Key Action Points from Yanelle's Story

- **Cultivate Curiosity:** Like Yanella, always be eager to learn and explore new ideas, industries, and cultures. This curiosity can connect you with diverse individuals who offer fresh perspectives and opportunities.
- **Seek Out Mentorship:** Don't hesitate to reach out to potential mentors who can help you navigate your industry. Yanella's relationship with Sophie Dubois was crucial in helping her understand the nuances of the Parisian fashion world.
- **Expand Your Network:** Attend industry events, join professional groups, and actively engage in communities aligned with your business interests. Building a robust network takes time, but it's essential for long-term success.
- **Be Selective in Partnerships:** Whether choosing an investor or a business partner, ensure they align with your values and vision. Yanella's strategic partnerships helped her maintain the integrity of her brand while achieving growth.

09. The Power of Niche Mastery and Strategic Alliances in Scaling a Business

In the journey of scaling a business, especially in competitive industries like digital marketing, mastering a specific niche and forming strategic alliances with industry leaders can provide a significant competitive advantage. This approach not only establishes your company as a leader in a specialised area but also opens doors to new opportunities and growth.

Raouf Bouaziz, a talented software engineer and entrepreneur originally from Haiti, had always been passionate about technology. After moving to Toronto, Canada, he saw an opportunity to address a specific pain point in the e-commerce industry: the inefficiency of inventory management for small to medium-sized businesses. Drawing from his experience in both software development and supply chain management, Raouf decided to launch his own company, OptiStock, a cloud-based inventory management platform.

Raouf understood the importance of focusing on a narrowly defined niche. He knew that small and medium-sized e-commerce businesses were often underserved by the big players in the industry, who typically catered to large enterprises with complex and costly solutions. Raouf's goal was to create a simple, affordable, and highly effective tool that could help these businesses manage their inventory more efficiently, thereby reducing costs and improving profitability.

In the beginning, Raouf's strategy was clear: become the best in this niche before considering any expansion. He dedicated himself to perfecting OptiStock's features, focusing on user-friendly design, seamless integration with popular e-commerce platforms, and real-time analytics. His relentless pursuit of excellence in this specific area quickly earned OptiStock a reputation as the go-to solution for small and medium-sized e-commerce companies in Toronto.

Raouf's big break came when he secured a strategic partnership with Shopify, a leading e-commerce platform headquartered in the same city. He had spent months networking within the local tech community, attending industry events, and engaging with key decision-makers at Shopify. Raouf's persistence paid off when Shopify recognized the value OptiStock could bring to their small business clients. The partnership not only provided OptiStock with increased visibility but also gave it the credibility that comes from being associated with a market leader.

As OptiStock's customer base grew, Raouf empowered his team by distributing accountability across various roles. He encouraged his employees to take ownership of their projects, fostering a culture of innovation and continuous improvement. This approach not only allowed Raouf to focus on strategic growth but also ensured that the company could scale effectively without sacrificing quality.

To maintain consistency as the business expanded, Raouf introduced systems and processes that standardised operations across the board. From customer support to product development, every aspect of the business was systemised to ensure that OptiStock could continue to deliver exceptional service, even as it grew.

Raouf's journey from a niche-focused startup to a recognised player in the e-commerce industry highlighted the power of strategic partnerships and the importance of becoming the best in a specific area before expanding. His success was a testament to the value of aligning with industry giants, empowering a capable team, and systemising operations for sustained growth.

Find established brands in your sector, align yourself with them, and become the best supplier to those brands.

Key Action Points from Raouf's Story

- **Start Niche, Then Expand:** Focus on mastering a specific niche where you can offer unparalleled value. Like Raouf, once your business is established as the best in that area, you can consider diversifying and expanding into new markets.
- **Form Strategic Partnerships:** Build alliances with industry leaders and key stakeholders. Understand their goals and demonstrate how your business can support them. Raouf's partnership with Shopify was pivotal in scaling OptiStock and gaining credibility.
- **Empower Your Team:** Encourage your team members to take ownership of their roles and contribute to the company's growth. Raouf's approach to distributing accountability helped foster innovation and allowed OptiStock to scale effectively.
- **Systemise for Consistency:** As your business grows, implement systems and processes that ensure consistency across operations. This structure will help maintain high standards while allowing for flexibility and innovation.

10. The Power of Resilience and Adaptability in Leadership

Resilience and adaptability are critical components of successful leadership, especially when faced with adversity. Leaders must learn to navigate challenges by continuously evolving, seeking strategic opportunities, and remaining committed to their vision, even when the path is unclear.

Fatou Diop, a visionary entrepreneur from Senegal, was known for her unwavering commitment to sustainable agriculture. Growing up in Dakar, she had seen firsthand the impact of climate change on local farming communities. After studying agronomy and business management in France, Fatou returned to Senegal with a mission: to create a social enterprise that would empower small-scale farmers with sustainable practices and access to international markets.

Fatou founded Teranga Farms, a cooperative that provided training in organic farming techniques and helped local farmers export their produce. The enterprise quickly gained traction, and Fatou became a respected leader in her community. However, success was not without its challenges. As Teranga Farms grew, Fatou faced significant obstacles, including political instability, fluctuating markets, and resistance from traditional farming methods.

One of the biggest tests of Fatou's leadership came when Teranga Farms was hit by a severe drought that devastated crops across the region. Many of the farmers were on the brink of losing everything, and the cooperative faced financial ruin. Fatou knew that the survival of Teranga Farms depended on her ability to navigate this crisis with resilience and adaptability.

Instead of succumbing to the pressure, Fatou saw the adversity as an opportunity to innovate. She began researching drought-resistant crops and new irrigation technologies that could mitigate the impact of climate change. She also reached out to an old friend, Maria Fernández, a Spanish agronomist she had met during her studies in France, who was now working for a global agricultural NGO. With Maria's help, Fatou secured a partnership with the NGO, which provided funding and technical support to implement these new solutions.

Fatou's ability to adapt and evolve Teranga Farms' strategy was pivotal. She introduced the new crops and irrigation systems to the cooperative, which not only saved the farmers' livelihoods but also made the cooperative more resilient to future climate challenges. Moreover, Fatou's leadership during the crisis solidified her reputation as a resilient and adaptable leader who could steer her organisation through the toughest of times.

As Teranga Farms recovered and even expanded its reach, Fatou reflected on the lessons she had learned. She realised that her willingness to embrace discomfort, her persistence in the face of failure, and her strategic approach to networking had been crucial in navigating the challenges she faced.

Sometimes we have to get terribly, terribly uncomfortable in order to become comfortable.

Key Action Points from Fatou's Story

- **Embrace Discomfort:** Like Fatou, recognise that true growth often comes from stepping outside of your comfort zone. When faced with adversity, embrace the challenge as an opportunity to develop new skills and perspectives.
- **Strategic Networking:** Build a network of advocates and allies who can support you in times of need. Fatou's partnership with Maria and the NGO was instrumental in overcoming the drought crisis.
- **Persistence Pays Off:** Don't be discouraged by setbacks or initial failures. Fatou's persistence, coupled with her strategic adjustments, allowed Teranga Farms to not only survive but thrive during a challenging time.
- **Adapt Your Communication:** Tailor your messaging to resonate with different audiences. Fatou's ability to communicate the benefits of new farming techniques to her cooperative members was key to their successful adoption.

11. Turning Frustration into Opportunity for Adaptability and Growth

In the journey of entrepreneurship, frustration often signals untapped opportunities. When traditional methods aren't yielding the desired results, it's crucial to listen carefully to what your market, clients, or environment is telling you. By adapting your strategy based on this feedback, you can transform obstacles into powerful opportunities for growth and success.

Jamal Campbell, a Caribbean entrepreneur from Jamaica, had always been passionate about technology and its potential to drive economic development in his home country. After studying software engineering abroad, Jamal returned to Kingston with a dream of building a tech startup that could empower small businesses across the island. He founded InnovateHub, a platform designed to help small and medium-sized enterprises (SMEs) digitise their operations, manage inventory, and reach customers online.

However, despite his enthusiasm and technical expertise, Jamal faced significant frustration in the early stages of his business. The adoption rate for InnovateHub was much lower than expected, and sales were not picking up as he had hoped. Jamal initially responded by ramping up his sales efforts, but this only led to more frustration. He realised that despite his best efforts, something fundamental was missing in his approach.

Instead of continuing down the same path, Jamal decided to take a step back and really listen to his potential clients. He scheduled meetings with several small business owners to understand their challenges and why they were hesitant to adopt InnovateHub's solutions. What he discovered was eye-opening: many business owners were overwhelmed by the complexity of digital tools and felt that the platform did not fully address their specific needs.

Armed with this new insight, Jamal decided to pivot. He simplified InnovateHub's interface, making it more user-friendly and tailored specifically to the needs of local businesses. He also introduced a series of workshops and one-on-one coaching sessions to help business owners understand the value of going digital and how to effectively use the platform.

This adaptive strategy quickly began to pay off. Business owners who had previously been sceptical started to see the value in InnovateHub, and word of mouth began to spread. Jamal's willingness to listen, adapt, and improve his offering based on client feedback transformed what was initially a source of frustration into a powerful growth opportunity.

As InnovateHub grew, so did its impact. Jamal's platform became a vital tool for SMEs in Kingston, helping them thrive in an increasingly digital world. His success was not just in creating a product but in building meaningful relationships with his clients and continually evolving his business to meet their needs.

Frustration in business is often a signal of untapped opportunity. By listening closely and adapting your strategy, you can turn challenges into success.

Key Action Points from Jamal's Story

- **Listen More, Sell Less:** Like Jamal, prioritise understanding your clients' real needs before offering solutions. Engage in meaningful conversations, ask the right questions, and listen attentively to uncover their true pain points.
- **Adapt Your Offering:** If your initial strategy isn't yielding results, don't be afraid to pivot. Modify your product, service, or messaging to better align with what your clients truly need, as Jamal did by simplifying InnovateHub and offering more hands-on support.
- **Continuous Improvement:** Use client feedback as a catalyst for refining your business strategies. This ongoing process of adaptation and improvement can lead to greater alignment with market demands and drive long-term success.
- **Build Relationships:** The strength of your business relationships is crucial. Invest time in developing these connections, as they can lead to referrals, repeat business, and opportunities that you might not have anticipated.

12. The Power of Strategic Partnerships and Willingness to Learn in Entrepreneurship

Strategic partnerships and a commitment to continuous learning are essential for sustained success in entrepreneurship. Building a successful business often requires more than just individual effort; it demands collaboration, leveraging networks, and being open to learning at every stage of the journey.

Moses Kato, a driven entrepreneur from Uganda, had always been passionate about using technology to solve social problems. After graduating with a degree in computer science, Moses moved to Nairobi, Kenya, with the dream of launching a tech startup that could address some of East Africa's most pressing issues. His initial idea was to create a platform that would connect small-scale farmers with markets, helping them get fair prices for their produce and reducing post-harvest losses.

Despite his technical expertise and a strong business plan, Moses soon realised that launching a successful startup would require more than just his individual effort. He faced numerous challenges, including limited access to funding, difficulties in navigating regulatory environments, and the need for market access. It became clear that strategic partnerships and continuous learning would be critical to his success.

Moses began by identifying gaps in his knowledge and resources. He realised that while he had the technical skills to build the platform, he needed help with securing government contracts and accessing larger markets. Recognising this, he sought out strategic partners who could complement his skills. One such partner was Priya Sharma, an experienced business consultant from India who had a deep understanding of the Kenyan market and strong connections with local government officials. Moses and Priya formed a partnership that allowed them to combine their strengths—Moses's technical expertise and Priya's market knowledge and connections.

Through their collaboration, Moses was able to secure a government contract that provided initial funding for his platform and access to a broader network of farmers. This partnership was instrumental in propelling his business forward, allowing him to scale his operations and increase his impact across the region.

In addition to leveraging partnerships, Moses committed himself to continuous learning. He regularly attended industry conferences, participated in online courses, and sought mentorship from seasoned entrepreneurs. This commitment to learning not only kept him informed about the latest industry trends but also equipped him with the knowledge to make strategic decisions as his business grew.

Moses also understood the importance of being adaptable. As the business evolved, he faced several challenges that required him to pivot his strategy. For instance, when the platform initially struggled to gain traction among farmers, Moses and his team decided to shift their focus to providing mobile financial services for small-scale farmers. This pivot proved successful, leading to rapid growth and a stronger value proposition for the platform.

Another key to Moses's success was his exploration of government and corporate contracts. While securing these contracts was complex and time-consuming, Moses understood the substantial rewards they could offer. By partnering with larger firms and targeting niche markets, Moses was able to build credibility and gain valuable experience, ultimately securing contracts that significantly boosted his business's growth.

True business success comes not from a single great idea, but from a constant journey of learning, cultivating, and adapting your approach.

Key Action Points from Moses's Story

- **Leverage Strategic Partnerships:** Like Moses, don't shy away from seeking partners who can complement your skills or resources. The right partnerships can significantly propel your business forward, as seen in his collaboration with Priya Sharma.
- **Embrace Continuous Learning:** Make learning a core part of your entrepreneurial journey. Moses's commitment to ongoing education and mentorship equipped him with the tools to make strategic decisions and stay ahead of industry trends.
- **Adapt and Pivot:** Be open to changing your business model or strategy based on new information or opportunities. Moses's decision to pivot to mobile financial services was key to his platform's success.
- **Explore Government and Corporate Contracts:** While securing these contracts can be complex and time-consuming, they offer substantial rewards. Moses's efforts to secure government contracts through strategic partnerships helped him scale his business significantly.

13. Navigating the Complexities of Identity and Success

This journey is a powerful testament to the importance of resilience, adaptability, and the relentless pursuit of one's goals. Nia's experience underscores that true success comes not just from professional achievements, but from aligning your values with your actions, embracing change, and turning adversity into strength.

Nia Amadou, a passionate and determined entrepreneur, grew up in Harlem, New York, but her roots trace back to the vibrant cultures of Senegal. Her parents, who had immigrated to the United States with dreams of a better life, instilled in Nia the values of hard work, perseverance, and cultural pride. Growing up in a multicultural household, Nia was exposed to a rich blend of traditions and perspectives, which shaped her outlook on life and business.

After completing her studies in computer science, Nia faced the harsh realities of the job market. Despite her qualifications, she encountered numerous obstacles, including racial bias and the challenges of being a woman in a male-dominated field. Rejection after rejection, Nia found herself at a crossroads. But instead of giving up, she decided to take control of her destiny. With a small amount of savings and a big dream, she moved to London to start her own tech consulting firm, specialising in digital transformation for small businesses.

In London, Nia's early days were filled with uncertainty. The market was competitive, and breaking through as an outsider was no easy feat. However, Nia's multicultural background and international outlook became her greatest assets. She leveraged her unique perspective to build a personal brand that resonated with a diverse clientele. Nia's ability to connect with people from all walks of life and her commitment to delivering high-quality results quickly set her apart.

One of Nia's first major clients was a mid-sized company struggling to transition to digital operations. The company had been burned by previous consultants who failed to understand their specific needs. Nia approached the project differently—she listened, adapted, and applied her deep understanding of both technology and human nature to create a tailored solution. Her efforts paid off, and the success of this project led to more opportunities, including partnerships with larger firms.

Throughout her journey, Nia faced moments of doubt and many setbacks. However, she embraced failure as a tool for learning and growth. Each mistake became a stepping stone, guiding her closer to success. She also recognised the importance of building a strong network, both locally and internationally. By aligning herself with mentors and peers who shared her vision, Nia was able to expand her influence and secure strategic partnerships that propelled her business forward.

As Nia's company grew, so did her impact. She became a mentor to young entrepreneurs, particularly women of colour, helping them navigate the challenges of the business world. For Nia, success was not just about financial gain but about making a meaningful difference in the lives of others.

Every single day is a blessing. The way I work every day is new and I don't dwell on what happened the day before.

Key Action Points from Nia's Story

- **Embrace Failure as a Learning Tool:** Like Nia, understand that failure is a natural part of the entrepreneurial journey. Use mistakes as opportunities to learn and grow, and don't let them deter you from pursuing your goals.
- **Leverage Personal Branding and Networking:** Success in a global market requires a strong personal brand and a robust network. Nia's ability to connect with diverse groups and build meaningful relationships was key to her business's success.
- **Persist Through Rejection:** Rejection is inevitable, but Nia's story teaches us the importance of persistence. View each "no" as the start of a conversation and an opportunity to refine your approach.
- **Focus on Impact and Authenticity:** True success lies in the balance between professional achievements and personal fulfilment. Nia's commitment to aligning her values with her actions and making a positive impact on others was central to her journey.

14. Mastering the Art of Strategic Growth Beyond the Basics

Success in business is not merely about doing the job well—it's about mastering how you do it and continuously challenging yourself to innovate, grow, and leverage relationships. Strategic growth demands a balance of excellence in execution, innovation, and personal leadership.

Elena Moya, a dynamic and ambitious Afro-Spanish marketing strategist, had always been passionate about creating impactful campaigns. Born and raised in Madrid, Spain, Elena was determined to make her mark in the world of marketing. After completing her studies, she landed a role at a prominent multinational company headquartered in Madrid. The job was highly competitive, with high expectations, but Elena was determined to excel.

From the beginning, Elena knew that standing out would require more than just meeting her job's requirements. She decided to focus on how she could bring innovation to her role. Rather than relying on traditional marketing methods, Elena began experimenting with new digital tools and data analytics to craft personalised campaigns that resonated with Spain's diverse audiences. Her innovative approach quickly distinguished her from her peers, catching the attention of senior leaders within the company.

Elena understood that success was not achieved in isolation. She made it a priority to build relationships within the organisation and the broader industry. She attended networking events, volunteered for cross-departmental projects, and actively sought out mentors. Her ability to forge meaningful connections paid off when she was recommended for a high-profile project that required close collaboration across multiple departments. Elena's strategic networking became a crucial factor in the project's success, showcasing her ability to work effectively with others.

Leadership, Elena knew, was not just about having a title. She took on mentoring roles, guiding junior colleagues and helping them navigate the complexities of their careers. When the company faced a major setback during a product launch, Elena stepped up to lead the crisis management efforts, even though it was outside her usual responsibilities. Her leadership during this challenging time demonstrated her ability to inspire and guide others, further solidifying her reputation as a leader within the company.

Despite her successes, Elena's journey was not without its challenges. There were times when she faced resistance to her ideas or encountered self-doubt. However, Elena's perseverance and belief in her vision allowed her to overcome these obstacles. She continued to push forward, refining her strategies and learning from every experience.

Elena's commitment to innovative execution, strategic networking, leadership, and perseverance led to her promotion to Regional Marketing Director for Southern Europe. Her journey from a marketing strategist to a senior leader in the company illustrates the power of going beyond expectations to achieve excellence.

Innovation in your approach and excellence in execution are the keys to unlocking strategic growth.

Key Action Points from Elena's Story

- **Emphasise the 'How':** Like Elena, regularly assess how you can innovate within your role. Look for ways to improve processes, strategies, and outcomes, and strive to add value beyond basic requirements.
- **Build and Leverage Your Network:** Engage in your organisation's networks and communities. Cultivate relationships with senior leaders and peers by being genuine, sharing your story, and contributing meaningfully to conversations.
- **Seek Opportunities for Leadership:** Don't wait for formal leadership roles to be handed to you. Actively seek out opportunities where you can demonstrate your ability to lead, mentor, and support others, as Elena did during the company's crisis.
- **Commit to Continuous Growth:** Regularly reflect on your career goals and take deliberate steps toward achieving them. Embrace big opportunities as chances to grow, even when they seem daunting.

15. Building Your Career Chessboard - Strategic Moves for Long-Term Success

Success in your career isn't just about excelling in your current role; it's about strategically positioning yourself for future opportunities. Like in chess, each move should be made with foresight, aiming not only to strengthen your present position but also to set the stage for your next big move.

Kwesi Thandeka, a driven and ambitious professional, had always been passionate about the intersection of finance and technology. Born and raised in Johannesburg, South Africa, Kwesi's journey was one of strategic planning, calculated risks, and a relentless pursuit of his career goals. After graduating with honours in finance from a top university, Kwesi landed his first job at a local bank, where he quickly became known for his analytical skills and work ethic.

However, Kwesi wasn't content with just doing his job well—he was always thinking several moves ahead. While his peers were focused on climbing the corporate ladder within the bank, Kwesi was already mapping out his future in the rapidly growing fintech industry. He knew that if he wanted to transition into this field, he needed to develop a different set of skills and experiences. Kwesi began by volunteering for projects that involved the bank's digital transformation efforts, even though they were outside his immediate responsibilities. These projects exposed him to cutting-edge financial technologies and allowed him to build relationships with key players in the fintech space. He also enrolled in online courses on coding and blockchain technology, investing in his own continuous learning.

Despite the long hours and additional workload, Kwesi remained focused on his future goals. His strategic efforts paid off when he was offered a position at a leading fintech startup in Cape Town. The move was risky—leaving the stability of his banking job for a startup environment—but Kwesi knew it was the right step for his long-term career. The startup provided him with the hands-on experience and industry insights he needed to solidify his expertise in fintech.

At the startup, Kwesi didn't just settle into his new role. He continued to think ahead, identifying emerging trends in the industry and positioning himself as an expert in those areas. His proactive approach led to him being promoted to a leadership position within two years, where he was responsible for spearheading new product innovations.

Kwesi's journey from a traditional finance role to a leadership position in fintech was a testament to the importance of strategic career planning. By thinking several steps ahead, optimising his current opportunities, and continuously investing in his growth, Kwesi successfully navigated his career towards his ultimate goals.

Don't just think about the job that you're doing now. Think about the job that you want to do after this.

Key Action Points from Kwesi's Story

- **Identify Future Goals:** Like Kwesi, spend time thinking about where you want to be in the next 5-10 years. Research the roles you aspire to and understand the qualifications and experiences needed to get there.
- **Optimise Current Opportunities:** Reflect on your current job and find ways to take on projects or responsibilities that will help you develop the skills required for your future roles. Kwesi's involvement in digital transformation projects helped him transition to fintech.
- **Invest in Continuous Learning:** Continuously seek out opportunities for professional development. Whether through online courses, certifications, or taking on new challenges, ensure you stay relevant and competitive in your field.
- **Build and Leverage Networks:** Establish and nurture connections with professionals who can offer guidance, mentorship, and opportunities aligned with your career goals. Kwesi's relationships in the fintech space were instrumental in his career transition.

16. Embracing Discomfort for Growth and Innovation

True growth and innovation in business occur when you embrace discomfort and step outside your comfort zone. By continuously pushing your boundaries, challenging the status quo, and staying curious, you position yourself and your organisation for long-term success.

Abiola Johnson, a dynamic African American woman in her mid-30s, had always been a high achiever. Born and raised in New York City, she had carved out a successful career in finance, working for a prestigious investment firm. Abiola was known for her analytical mind and her ability to close deals, but she was also recognized for her leadership potential. However, despite her success, Abiola felt a sense of complacency creeping in. She was comfortable in her role but knew deep down that she wasn't growing or challenging herself in the way she had envisioned.

One day, Abiola's firm announced an opportunity to lead a new initiative—launching their first international office in Lagos, Nigeria. The role was highly coveted, but it also came with significant risks. Lagos was a rapidly growing market, but it was also unfamiliar territory for the firm, full of challenges ranging from navigating local regulations to understanding cultural nuances. Many of Abiola's colleagues hesitated to apply, seeing the role as a potential career risk. But for Abiola, this was exactly the kind of discomfort she had been yearning for.

Determined to push her boundaries, Abiola applied for the position and was selected to lead the expansion. This decision was met with mixed reactions. Some colleagues praised her bravery, while others quietly questioned her judgement. Abiola knew the road ahead would be tough, but she also knew that embracing this discomfort was essential for her growth.

Upon arriving in Lagos, Abiola faced a steep learning curve. The business environment was different from what she was used to—relationships mattered more than just numbers, and understanding the local culture was crucial to success. She had to quickly adapt to new ways of working, often stepping into situations that were uncomfortable and unfamiliar.

Abiola's first major challenge was negotiating a partnership with a leading Nigerian bank. The deal was critical to establishing the firm's presence in the market. However, the negotiations were complex, involving multiple stakeholders with varying interests. Abiola felt the pressure but remained focused. She leaned on her curiosity to understand the local business dynamics and sought advice from local mentors who had successfully navigated similar challenges.

Despite the initial discomfort, Abiola's willingness to embrace these challenges paid off. She approached the negotiations not just with her usual analytical skills but with a deep respect for the local culture, building trust with her Nigerian counterparts. This approach led to a successful partnership that not only solidified the firm's presence in Lagos but also exceeded the firm's expectations in terms of profitability and growth.

Throughout her time in Nigeria, Abiola continued to embrace discomfort as a catalyst for innovation. She explored new technologies that were transforming the African financial landscape, such as mobile banking and fintech solutions. By staying curious and continuously learning, she was able to position her firm as a leader in this emerging market.

Abiola's journey in Lagos transformed her into a more confident and innovative leader. She returned to New York with a wealth of new experiences, ready to take on even bigger challenges.

Abiola's story is a powerful reminder that true growth and innovation come from stepping outside your comfort zone. By embracing discomfort, staying curious, and leveraging her network, Abiola not only advanced her career but also drove significant value for her organisation.

Your comfort zone is a lovely place to be, but nothing grows there.

Key Action Points from Abiola's Story

- **Seek Discomfort:** Like Abiola, actively pursue roles and challenges that push you out of your comfort zone. Growth happens when you're slightly uneasy.
- **Cultivate Curiosity:** Abiola's success was fueled by her curiosity and willingness to learn about new markets and technologies. Stay curious to stay ahead.
- **Leverage Your Network:** Building relationships with local mentors and industry experts was key to Abiola's success in Lagos. Leverage your network for guidance and support.
- **Focus on Value Creation:** Align your efforts with the core needs of your organisation. Abiola's focus on understanding the local market and adding value led to a successful expansion.

17. The Power of Character and Resilience in Business Success

In the pursuit of business success, hiring for character, competence, and resilience is just as crucial as technical skills. Beyond qualifications and experience, these qualities ensure that team members will persevere through challenges, maintain integrity, and consistently deliver results.

Mariam Idriss, a determined entrepreneur originally from Chad, had made London her home and the base for her business operations. After moving to the UK to pursue higher education, Mariam developed a deep interest in sustainable fashion and decided to start her own ethical fashion brand in the heart of the city. Her vision was not just to create beautiful, sustainable clothing but to empower women from underrepresented communities by providing them with fair employment opportunities.

Mariam knew that the success of her business depended heavily on the team she built. While technical skills in design and production were important, Mariam understood that character, competence, and resilience were equally crucial. She needed team members who could handle the pressures of a startup environment, maintain integrity in their work, and show resilience in the face of the challenges that come with being a small business in a competitive market like London.

During the hiring process, Mariam focused on more than just the resumes in front of her. She asked potential employees situational questions designed to reveal their character and resilience. For example, she asked how they had handled previous failures or ethical dilemmas, and how they managed stress in high-pressure situations. One candidate, Amina, shared a story about how she had navigated a difficult situation in a previous job, where she had to balance the demands of an intense work environment with maintaining her integrity and supporting her colleagues. Impressed by Amina's experience and outlook, Mariam hired her as the head of production.

As the business grew, Mariam fostered a culture of integrity and resilience within her team. She led by example, always keeping her promises and encouraging open communication. Whenever challenges arose, whether it was a supply chain issue or a tight deadline, Mariam worked closely with her team to find solutions, often using these moments as opportunities for growth. She encouraged her employees to take ownership of their roles, instilling in them the confidence that they could overcome any obstacles.

Mariam also made it a priority to build resilience within her team. She assigned challenging projects that pushed her employees out of their comfort zones but provided them with the support and resources needed to succeed. For instance, when a large order came in from a high-profile retailer, Mariam entrusted Amina and the team with the responsibility to manage the project from start to finish. The experience was challenging, but it ultimately strengthened the team's confidence and cohesion.

Regular evaluations of both performance and character became a key part of Mariam's leadership approach. She held one-on-one meetings with her team members, providing constructive feedback and identifying areas for further development. These evaluations weren't just about assessing work output but also about nurturing the resilience and integrity that Mariam valued so highly.

Mariam's focus on hiring and nurturing employees with strong character and resilience paid off. Her business not only survived the typical struggles of a startup but thrived, gaining recognition in the sustainable fashion industry and securing partnerships with major retailers.

Success is built on the shoulders of those who not only have the skills but also the character and resilience to weather the storms and still deliver.

Key Action Points from Mariam's Story

- **Hire Beyond the Resume:** Like Mariam, assess potential employees not just for their qualifications but also for their resilience and character. Use situational interview questions to understand how they handle stress, failure, and ethical dilemmas.
- **Foster a Culture of Integrity:** Encourage an environment where promises are kept, and employees take ownership of their roles. Lead by example and maintain open communication to build trust and accountability.
- **Build Resilience:** Create opportunities for employees to build resilience, such as through challenging projects or allowing them to learn from failures. Support them with the necessary resources and encouragement to grow from these experiences.
- **Evaluate Regularly:** Regularly assess the character and resilience of your team members, not just their performance. Provide feedback and development opportunities to strengthen these areas, ensuring a robust and dependable workforce.

18. The Power of Resilience and Strategic Patience in Career Advancement

Success in your career often hinges on resilience, strategic patience, and continuous learning. It's essential to believe in yourself, navigate challenges with a clear vision, and strategically position yourself for opportunities, even when the path seems unclear or obstacles arise.

Kassim Mbemba, a Congolese professional, had always been driven by a desire to make a meaningful impact in the business world. After completing his education in Kinshasa, Kassim moved to Toronto, Canada, with high hopes of advancing his career in finance. Toronto, known for its diverse and competitive job market, presented numerous opportunities, but Kassim quickly realised that the road to success would not be straightforward.

Despite his qualifications, Kassim faced numerous challenges in securing a job that matched his skills and ambitions. The competitive nature of the financial industry in Toronto meant that opportunities were scarce, and Kassim found himself starting in a position that was far below his capabilities. It was a humbling experience, but Kassim knew that success required resilience and strategic patience.

Kassim embraced his initial setbacks as learning opportunities. He understood that career growth is not always linear, and sometimes, lateral moves or even temporary setbacks are necessary to eventually move forward. Kassim focused on expanding his knowledge and skills by enrolling in additional finance courses and earning certifications that would strengthen his expertise. He also took the time to learn about the Canadian financial industry, understanding its unique challenges and opportunities.

During this time, Kassim also focused on building strong relationships within the industry. He attended networking events, joined professional associations, and sought out mentors who could provide guidance and support. One such mentor, Sarah Chang, a senior executive at a major financial firm, recognised Kassim's potential and offered him invaluable advice on navigating the industry. With Sarah's guidance, Kassim learned the importance of positioning himself strategically and being patient as he waited for the right opportunity to arise.

Kassim's hard work and resilience eventually paid off. After several years of perseverance, he was offered a role as a financial analyst at a top firm, a position that aligned with his long-term goals. The experience he had gained, coupled with his continuous learning and strategic networking, positioned him as a strong candidate for the role. His journey was a testament to the power of believing in oneself and the importance of resilience and strategic planning in overcoming obstacles.

As Kassim continued to advance in his career, he remained committed to his principles of resilience, continuous learning, and strategic patience. He understood that success was not just about reaching the top quickly but about building a sustainable and fulfilling career.

You have to believe in yourself. You have to be your number one fan. No one is going to do it for you.

Key Action Points from Kassim's Story

- **Embrace Resilience:** Like Kassim, understand that setbacks are a part of the journey. Rather than viewing them as failures, see them as opportunities to learn, adapt, and come back stronger.
- **Invest in Continuous Learning:** Continuously seek to expand your knowledge and skills. Kassim's decision to pursue additional finance courses and certifications kept him relevant in his field and equipped him to pivot when necessary.
- **Build Strong Relationships:** Cultivate a network of reliable and supportive contacts. Kassim's relationship with his mentor, Sarah Chang, was instrumental in guiding his career and helping him navigate the complexities of the financial industry in Toronto.
- **Be Strategic and Patient:** Recognise that career growth takes time. Be patient, but also be proactive in seeking out opportunities that align with your long-term goals. Kassim's strategic patience allowed him to wait for the right role that matched his aspirations.

19. The Path to Business Growth and Success

In the world of business, adaptability and the willingness to embrace change are critical for growth and success. Entrepreneurs often face crossroads where staying in a comfortable position or pushing boundaries becomes a pivotal decision. True progress requires stepping outside of comfort zones, re-evaluating strategies, and being open to new opportunities.

Marie Thompson, a trailblazing African American entrepreneur, stood on the rooftop of her tech startup's headquarters in Melbourne, Australia. The city, with its eclectic blend of cultures and forward-thinking vibe, had become a fertile ground for innovation. Marie had moved to Melbourne five years ago after selling her first company in New York—a boutique digital marketing firm that had become a leader in its niche. But as much as she loved her success, Marie knew it was time for a new challenge.

Marie's decision to relocate to Melbourne wasn't just about geography; it was about redefining her career path. She had always believed in the power of technology to drive social change, and Melbourne's burgeoning tech scene offered the perfect environment to explore this vision. Her new venture, a platform designed to connect small businesses with digital tools and resources, was inspired by her desire to empower entrepreneurs in underserved communities.

However, starting over in a new country was no easy feat. Marie faced significant challenges, from navigating a different business landscape to building a network from scratch. But she was undeterred. Drawing from her experience, she knew that growth required stepping out of her comfort zone and embracing the unknown.

Marie's big break came when she met Wei Zhang, a prominent Chinese-Australian investor, at a tech innovation summit. Wei was intrigued by Marie's platform, not only because of its potential for scalability but also because of the social impact it promised. Unlike many other pitches, Marie's vision wasn't just about profit—it was about making a difference in communities that were often overlooked.

Recognising an opportunity to learn from someone with deep local insights, Marie cultivated a relationship with Wei. They collaborated on several initiatives aimed at integrating small businesses into the digital economy, with Marie's platform at the forefront. This partnership, coupled with her relentless drive, allowed Marie to secure significant investment and expand her platform across the Asia-Pacific region.

As her company grew, Marie made a conscious effort to build a diverse team that reflected her commitment to inclusivity. Her employees came from various ethnic backgrounds, bringing a wide range of perspectives and ideas. This diversity became one of the company's greatest strengths, fueling innovation and helping the business to connect with a broader audience.

Marie's journey in Melbourne was a testament to the importance of adaptability and the courage to pursue new opportunities, even when the path wasn't clear. By moving on from her previous success, she opened doors to new possibilities and made a meaningful impact in the process.

I don't want to spend the next five years doing what I spent the last five years doing. You have to make yourself redundant in your role to grow and take on new challenges.

Key Action Points from Marie's Story

- **Embrace Change for Growth:** Like Marie, don't hesitate to leave a thriving position or business if it no longer aligns with your evolving goals. This willingness to embrace change can lead to new opportunities and greater success.
- **Leverage Cultural Diversity:** Surround yourself with a team that brings diverse perspectives and experiences. This not only fosters innovation but also allows your business to connect with a broader audience.
- **Cultivate Strategic Partnerships:** Seek out partnerships that offer more than just financial backing. Collaborating with individuals who share your vision and can provide local insights, as Marie did with Wei, can significantly enhance your chances of success in new markets.
- **Prioritise Social Impact:** Consider how your business can make a positive impact on society. Building a company with a strong social mission, like Marie's platform, can differentiate your brand and attract both investors and customers who share your values.

20. The Strategic Advantage of Content Driven Growth

Creating and leveraging content is a powerful strategy for career and business growth. It's not just about producing material; it's about creating content that resonates with your audience's needs, showcases your expertise, and positions you as a thought leader in your industry.

Noura Khaled, an Egyptian-born marketing strategist, had always been fascinated by the power of storytelling. After completing her studies in Cairo, she moved to Berlin, Germany, to pursue a career in digital marketing. Berlin, with its vibrant tech scene and diverse culture, was the perfect place for Noura to explore innovative marketing strategies. However, as she started her career in a new city, she quickly realised that standing out in a competitive market would require more than just traditional marketing tactics.

Noura knew that to build her brand and establish herself as an expert in the field, she needed to leverage content in a way that resonated with her target audience. She began by researching the needs, challenges, and interests of the businesses she wanted to work with. Noura discovered that many startups in Berlin were struggling with building an authentic online presence that connected with their audience on a deeper level.

With this insight, Noura started creating content that addressed these specific challenges. She wrote blog posts, created infographics, and produced short videos that provided actionable tips on building brand authenticity and engaging customers effectively. Her content was not only informative but also tailored to the unique needs of the Berlin startup scene.

Noura's consistency in producing high-quality, relevant content quickly paid off. Her blog gained traction, and she began to attract the attention of industry leaders and potential clients. Noura used her content as a conversation starter, reaching out to key players in the tech community and sharing her insights. These interactions led to collaborations, speaking engagements, and consulting opportunities.

As Noura's reputation grew, she continuously evaluated the impact of her content. She paid close attention to engagement metrics, feedback from her audience, and the success of the strategies she shared. Noura used this data to refine her content strategy, ensuring it remained aligned with the evolving needs of her audience.

Through her content-driven approach, Noura established herself as a thought leader in the Berlin marketing scene. Her ability to create content that resonated with her audience not only boosted her career but also helped her build a successful consulting business, where she now advises startups on effective content strategies.

If you have content that people want to see that people find valuable, meaning you have to do enough due diligence to understand what they find valuable.

Key Action Points from Noura's Story

- **Start with Research:** Like Noura, invest time in understanding your audience's needs, challenges, and interests before creating content. This ensures that your content is relevant and valuable, positioning you as an expert in your field.
- **Consistency is Key:** Regularly produce and share content that aligns with your expertise. Whether it's through blogs, articles, presentations, or podcasts, consistent content creation helps build your brand and authority.
- **Leverage Content to Build Relationships:** Use your content as a conversation starter with clients, colleagues, and industry leaders. Noura's content opened doors to new opportunities and partnerships in the Berlin startup scene.
- **Measure Impact and Adjust:** Continuously evaluate the impact of your content. Use feedback and engagement metrics to refine your strategy and ensure it remains aligned with your goals, just as Noura did throughout her journey.

21. The Power of Strategic Networking and Continuous Learning in Business Success

Strategic networking and continuous learning are crucial components for advancing in any industry. These elements not only enhance personal growth but also open doors to new opportunities and resources that can significantly impact your career trajectory.

Burhaan Jamac, a driven entrepreneur originally from Somalia, moved to Dubai with the ambition of establishing herself in the competitive world of tech startups. Dubai's dynamic business environment and global connections offered Burhaan the perfect platform to bring her ideas to life, but she quickly realised that to succeed, she would need more than just a great product. She needed to strategically network and continuously learn in an ever-evolving industry.

Burhaan's initial months in Dubai were challenging. Despite her technical expertise and innovative ideas, she struggled to gain traction in a market dominated by established players. However, Burhaan understood that success in business was often determined by the relationships you cultivate and the knowledge you acquire over time. With this insight, she decided to focus on two key strategies: strategic networking and continuous learning.

Burhaan began attending industry conferences, tech meetups, and business forums, not just to pitch her startup but to build genuine relationships with other professionals. She networked with intention, seeking out mentors, potential collaborators, and industry veterans who could offer guidance and share their experiences. One of these connections was Rahul Kapoor, a seasoned tech entrepreneur from India who had successfully launched multiple startups in the Middle East. Rahul was impressed by Burhaan's vision and offered to mentor her, providing insights into the local market and introducing her to key players in the industry.

In parallel with her networking efforts, Burhaan committed to continuous learning. She enrolled in online courses to expand her knowledge of digital marketing and business management, knowing that these skills would be crucial as she scaled her startup. She also regularly engaged with thought leaders through podcasts, webinars, and industry publications to stay informed about the latest trends and innovations in the tech world.

Burhaan embraced the role of a learner, even when working alongside seasoned professionals. She approached every meeting, project, and partnership with an open mind, always eager to learn something new. This humility and willingness to absorb knowledge differentiated her in the competitive tech landscape.

Over time, Burhaan's strategic networking and commitment to learning began to pay off. With Rahul's mentorship and the connections she had built, she was able to secure funding for her startup and gain access to resources that accelerated her company's growth. Additionally, her continuous learning efforts allowed her to pivot and adapt her business model in response to market demands, positioning her startup for long-term success.

Burhaan also understood the importance of playing her position effectively within her team. While she was the visionary behind the startup, she recognised the value of being a supportive leader who empowered her team members to excel in their roles. This approach fostered a collaborative environment where everyone contributed to the company's success.

Networking is not just about building contacts; it's about building relationships that enrich your career and life.

Key Action Points from Burhaan's Story

- **Build Relationships with Purpose:** Like Hodan, network with the intention of forming genuine relationships rather than seeking immediate benefits. Focus on connecting with individuals who can offer guidance, share knowledge, and inspire you to grow.
- **Stay Curious and Keep Learning:** Dedicate time to continuous learning, whether through formal education, listening to industry podcasts, or engaging with thought leaders. Hodan's commitment to learning kept her informed and adaptable in a rapidly changing business environment.
- **Embrace the Role of a Learner:** Whether you are at the start of your career or a seasoned professional, always approach new opportunities with a learner's mindset. Hodan's humility and openness to new ideas differentiated her in the tech industry.
- **Play Your Position Effectively:** Understand the value of being a supportive team member. Not everyone needs to be the leader; sometimes, the most significant impact comes from being a strong number two or three. Hodan's leadership style focused on empowering her team, which contributed to the startup's success.

22. The Power of Strategic Patience in Career Advancement

In career advancement, particularly within large organisations, the importance of strategic patience cannot be overstated. While short-term decisions can often be made quickly, long-term career decisions require careful thought, planning, and the cultivation of key relationships.

Leila Alleyne, a determined and talented professional originally from Barbados, had always dreamed of making her mark in the corporate world. After earning her degree in economics, Leila moved to London, where she landed a coveted role at a top consulting firm. The fast-paced environment of London was a far cry from the laid-back rhythm of her island home, but Leila was eager to prove herself and excel.

As she navigated the competitive corporate landscape, Leila quickly made a name for herself with her sharp analytical skills and relentless work ethic. However, after a few years, she found herself at a crossroads. Many of her peers were jumping to new companies, chasing promotions and higher salaries, but Leila sensed that her long-term success might require a different approach—one rooted in strategic patience.

Despite receiving tempting offers from other firms, Leila chose to stay with her current company. She understood that the relationships she had built and the knowledge she had gained were invaluable assets that could be leveraged for greater opportunities in the future. Leila also recognised the importance of aligning her work with the firm's long-term goals. She began to focus on projects that were not only challenging but also highly visible to the firm's leadership.

Leila was fortunate to find a mentor in James Mitchell, a senior partner at the firm who had a reputation for making strategic decisions with precision. James saw potential in Leila and took her under his wing, teaching her the importance of patience in career growth. He advised her to think carefully about her long-term goals and to make decisions that would position her for sustained success.

Under James's mentorship, Leila began to view her career as a long game. Instead of making impulsive moves for short-term gains, she strategically took on roles and projects that aligned with her vision of becoming a leader in the firm. She worked on initiatives that had a significant impact on the company's bottom line and positioned herself as someone who could drive long-term value.

Over time, Leila's strategic patience paid off. While her peers moved frequently between companies, Leila steadily advanced within her firm. She built a robust network, gained valuable experience, and earned the trust and respect of senior leaders. When a senior management position opened up, Leila was the natural choice. Her careful, deliberate approach had not only positioned her for the role but had also ensured that she was ready to excel in it.

Never rush long-term decisions. Take your time to really ensure that you are thinking strategically about them. Short-term decisions—you could make those decisions at any time.

Key Action Points from Leila's Story

- **Cultivate Patience:** Like Leila, avoid rushing decisions that will impact your long-term career. Take the time to evaluate your options, assess your goals, and ensure that any major moves align with your long-term vision.
- **Build Strong Relationships:** Identify and nurture relationships with sponsors and mentors within your organisation. Leila's relationship with James Mitchell was crucial in guiding her career and helping her navigate the complexities of her firm.
- **Focus on Strategic Impact:** Continuously think about how your work adds value to the organisation. Leila's focus on aligning her efforts with the company's broader goals positioned her as a leader in driving strategic initiatives.
- **Seek Feedback and Adapt:** Regularly seek feedback on your performance and areas for growth. Use this feedback to refine your approach and address any gaps that could hinder your progression, just as Leila did throughout her career.

23. The Power of Persistence and Planning in Business Growth

In the world of business, persistence and meticulous planning are crucial for long-term success. These elements not only shape a business strategy but also define the journey of an entrepreneur. The path to success is rarely straightforward, and those who achieve it often do so by embracing challenges, adapting to circumstances, and maintaining a clear vision.

Elodie Mbaye, an ambitious entrepreneur from Mauritius, always dreamed of making a mark in the international business world. After completing her education in business management, she moved to Singapore, a bustling hub of innovation and commerce, to start her entrepreneurial journey. Armed with passion and a clear vision, Elodie launched her first venture—a small import-export business focused on bringing unique Mauritian products to the Asian market.

However, the road was far from smooth. In the early stages, Elodie faced numerous challenges, including navigating the complexities of international trade, fierce competition, and the need to build brand recognition in a foreign market. Despite these setbacks, Elodie was determined to succeed. She understood that persistence and meticulous planning were key to overcoming these obstacles and achieving long-term success.

Elodie began by embracing persistence. She refused to be disheartened by the initial struggles, knowing that setbacks were a natural part of the entrepreneurial journey. With her long-term goals in sight, she adjusted her strategies as necessary, continuously refining her business model to better meet the needs of her target market.

Understanding the value of transferable skills, Elodie invested time in developing her expertise in sales, financial planning, and organisation. She knew that these skills would be crucial as she navigated different industries and roles. Her ability to adapt and apply these skills in various contexts allowed her to pivot her business model when needed, ultimately leading to greater success.

Financial literacy was another area where Elodie placed significant emphasis. She recognised early on that managing and growing her financial assets was essential for building a sustainable business. Seeking advice from financial advisors, Elodie learned how to manage her finances effectively, ensuring that her business had a strong financial foundation. This planning not only helped her weather tough economic times but also positioned her company for future growth.

Elodie's focus on long-term planning and persistence eventually paid off. Her import-export business began to gain traction, securing contracts with major retailers across Asia. Her success allowed her to expand her operations, bringing more products from Mauritius and even exploring new markets.

Through her journey, Elodie learned the importance of planning for longevity. She shifted her mindset from seeking short-term gains to focusing on long-term wealth creation. This approach ensured that her decisions were not just about immediate success but about building a legacy for future generations.

Success in business is about showing up consistently, planning meticulously, and never giving up, no matter how tough the journey gets.

Key Action Points from Elodie's Story

- **Embrace Persistence:** Like Elodie, don't be disheartened by early setbacks or initial failures. Keep your long-term goals in sight and persistently work towards them, adjusting your strategies as necessary.
- **Develop Transferable Skills:** Cultivate skills like sales, financial planning, and organisation, which can be applied across various roles and industries. These will prove invaluable as you progress in your career.
- **Invest in Financial Literacy:** Understand that financial management is not just for the wealthy. Start learning and seeking advice on how to manage and grow your assets early on to build a strong financial foundation.
- **Plan for Longevity:** Shift your mindset from short-term gains to long-term wealth creation. Think beyond your immediate needs and consider how your decisions will impact your future and the future of generations to come.

24. Leveraging Unconventional Opportunities for Career Growth

In today's competitive landscape, success often hinges on the ability to recognise and seize unconventional opportunities. These opportunities can arise in unexpected places, and being prepared to pivot or explore new avenues can significantly enhance career progression and personal development.

Idris Saleh, a driven professional originally from Libya, had always been passionate about technology and innovation. After earning his degree in engineering, Idris worked for several years in Tripoli, where he gained experience in the oil and gas industry. However, political instability and a desire for new challenges led him to consider opportunities abroad. When a chance opportunity to move to New Zealand arose, Idris decided to take the leap, even though it meant stepping into an entirely new environment and industry.

Moving to Auckland, New Zealand, was a significant change for Idris. The landscape, culture, and industry were all vastly different from what he had known in Libya. But Idris understood that career growth is not always linear, and sometimes, the most valuable opportunities come from areas you might not initially consider. He was determined to make the most of this new chapter in his life.

Upon arriving in Auckland, Idris quickly realised that the tech industry was booming, with significant opportunities in renewable energy—a field that piqued his interest. Despite his background in oil and gas, Idris decided to pivot into the renewable energy sector. He began by attending industry conferences, networking events, and engaging with professionals in the field. This proactive approach allowed him to build a strong network in a relatively short period of time.

Idris's willingness to embrace flexibility and adapt to a new industry paid off. Through his networking efforts, he secured a position with a leading renewable energy company in Auckland. His engineering skills were transferable, but he knew he needed to invest in continuous learning to fully transition into his new role. Idris enrolled in courses on renewable energy technologies and sustainability, quickly gaining the knowledge necessary to succeed in his new field.

As he settled into his role, Idris didn't stop challenging the status quo. He proposed innovative solutions to optimise the company's energy projects, drawing on his diverse background and fresh perspective. His ideas were well-received, and Idris soon found himself leading a team tasked with implementing new technologies that positioned the company as a leader in the industry.

Idris's story is a testament to the power of recognising and seizing unconventional opportunities. By stepping outside his comfort zone, leveraging his network, and committing to continuous learning, Idris not only navigated a successful career pivot but also positioned himself as a forward-thinking leader in his new industry.

Recognise those opportunities when they come. Being exposed to new people, new places, and being in important rooms can transform your career.

Key Action Points from Idris's Story

- **Embrace Flexibility:** Like Idris, be open to exploring new opportunities, even if they seem unconventional. Flexibility and adaptability are key to navigating a rapidly changing career landscape.
- **Leverage Networking:** Actively seek out and engage in networking opportunities, both within and outside your industry. Idris's networking efforts in Auckland were crucial in helping him secure a position in a new industry.
- **Invest in Continuous Learning:** Take advantage of every opportunity to learn, whether through formal education, new job experiences, or personal projects. Idris's commitment to learning allowed him to transition successfully into the renewable energy sector.
- **Challenge the Status Quo:** Don't be afraid to question existing norms and explore innovative solutions. Idris's willingness to propose new ideas helped him establish himself as a leader in his field.

25. A Strategic Approach to Success and Building Confidence

In any professional journey, the key to success lies in leveraging your strengths rather than dwelling on what you lack. By focusing on what you can offer and how you can provide value, you position yourself for growth and advancement, even in environments where you may initially feel out of place.

Thandi Chirwa, a young and driven professional hailing from Malawi, had always been fueled by a deep sense of ambition. After successfully completing her degree in international business, she embarked on a new chapter in Johannesburg, South Africa, with high hopes of making a substantial impact within the corporate world. Johannesburg, known for its vibrant and fast-paced business environment, initially felt like a whirlwind to Thandi. She quickly became aware that many of her peers enjoyed advantages she didn't—be it through well-established networks, prestigious educational backgrounds, or substantial financial resources.

It would have been easy for Thandi to dwell on these disparities and feel discouraged. However, instead of succumbing to feelings of inadequacy, she made a conscious decision to focus on her own strengths and unique attributes. Thandi was well-regarded for her exceptional work ethic, her remarkable ability to build connections with individuals from diverse backgrounds, and her profound understanding of African markets—an area in which she had considerable expertise. Determined to make a meaningful impact, Thandi resolved to make these qualities the foundation of her approach to her new role at a leading multinational firm.

From the outset, Thandi concentrated on how she could contribute value to her team. During meetings and strategy sessions, she leveraged her deep insights into emerging markets across Africa, a region she knew intimately. Her colleagues soon recognized the significant depth of her knowledge and began to rely on her for strategic guidance and advice.

Thandi's ability to build strong relationships with clients and accurately gauge their needs also distinguished her from her peers. She wasn't merely fulfilling her job requirements; she was continuously seeking ways to enhance value for both her team and the company at large.

Despite the initial discomfort and feelings of being out of place, Thandi consciously chose not to compare herself to others. She understood that everyone's journey was unique and that her path was just beginning to unfold. Rather than fixating on the advantages her peers possessed, she directed her energy towards her own strengths and how she could utilize them to advance her career.

As Thandi progressively applied her strengths, her confidence grew exponentially. She began to take on more significant projects, spearheaded various initiatives, and played a pivotal role in her company's expansion into new African markets. Her consistent and valuable contributions did not go unnoticed. Over time, Thandi earned the respect and trust of both her colleagues and senior management, solidifying her position as a key player in the company.

Thandi's journey, marked by resilience and a strategic focus on her unique strengths, exemplified how determination and self-awareness could lead to remarkable achievements, even in the face of initial challenges. Her story serves as a testament to the power of leveraging one's inherent capabilities and persisting through the complexities of a competitive environment.

If you walk into any situation focusing on what you don't have, then you're never going to make it.

Key Action Points from Thandi's Story

- **Identify Your Strengths:** Like Thandi, take time to understand what you excel at. Whether it's a specific skill, work ethic, or your ability to connect with others, make these strengths the cornerstone of your professional approach.
- **Focus on Value Creation:** Always think about how you can help or add value in any situation. Thandi's focus on delivering unique insights and connecting with clients allowed her strengths to shine through her contributions.
- **Avoid Comparisons:** Resist the urge to compare yourself to others, especially in terms of what you lack. Thandi's success came from focusing on her journey rather than dwelling on the advantages others had.
- **Build Confidence Through Action:** Confidence comes from consistent action. The more you focus on delivering value through your strengths, the more confident you will become in your abilities, just as Thandi did.

26. Understanding Your Customers and Target Audience for Business Success

In business, understanding your customers is not just a nice-to-have; it is a fundamental requirement for long-term success. Knowing who your best customers are, what their journey looks like, and how to meet their needs effectively can be the difference between thriving and merely surviving in a competitive market.

Amina Deng, a determined entrepreneur from South Sudan, moved to Amsterdam, Netherlands, with the dream of creating a unique hospitality business that catered to travellers looking for a personalised and culturally rich experience. After years of working in the hospitality industry in various countries, Amina was ready to take on the challenge of starting her own boutique hotel in a bustling European city.

From the very beginning, Amina understood that the key to her success in Amsterdam's competitive market would be a deep understanding of her customers. She knew that her most loyal and profitable guests would not be just any travellers but those who sought out authentic, culturally immersive experiences. Amina made it a priority to identify and analyse her best customers—those who returned to her hotel, left positive reviews, and recommended her hotel to others.

Amina engaged with her guests directly, gathering insights into their preferences and understanding what made them choose her hotel over others. She discovered that many of her guests were cultural enthusiasts, professionals attending conferences, and travellers looking for a more personalised stay compared to the generic experiences offered by larger hotel chains. These guests valued the unique South Sudanese influences Amina incorporated into her hotel's decor, cuisine, and hospitality.

To take her customer understanding to the next level, Amina leveraged data effectively. She implemented a robust data collection system that tracked guest preferences, booking patterns, and feedback. This data allowed her to tailor her services even more precisely to her customers' needs, offering personalised experiences that kept them coming back.

Amina also recognised the importance of focusing on customer retention. She developed strategies to retain her existing customer base, such as offering loyalty programs, personalised communication, and special events that catered to her guests' interests. These efforts not only strengthened her relationships with her guests but also helped her stand out in a crowded market.

To ensure that her entire team was aligned in delivering a seamless customer experience, Amina fostered cross-departmental collaboration within her hotel.

She encouraged her staff—from the front desk to housekeeping—to share insights and work together to anticipate and meet guests' needs. This unified approach created a consistent and exceptional experience for every guest, reinforcing their loyalty to Amina's hotel.

Begin by identifying your customers and mapping out their experiences to guide your path forward.

Key Action Points from Amina's Story

- **Identify and Analyse Your Best Customers:** Like Amina, understand who your most loyal and profitable customers are. Examine their journey from first contact to becoming a loyal customer, and understand what differentiates them from less engaged customers.
- **Leverage Data Effectively:** Use data to gain insights into customer behaviour, preferences, and needs. Ensure that your data collection and analysis processes are robust and integrated across departments to provide a complete view of your customers.
- **Focus on Customer Retention:** Don't just chase new customers. Develop strategies to retain your existing customer base by continually meeting their needs and exceeding their expectations.
- **Foster Cross-Departmental Collaboration:** Ensure that different departments within your organisation work together with a unified approach to understanding and serving your customers. Align objectives and share insights across teams to create a seamless customer experience.

27. The Power of Resilience and Adaptability in Leadership

Mastering a specific skill and sharing it with the world can open doors to diverse opportunities, transforming your expertise into a powerful asset. By focusing on one area and becoming exceptionally skilled in it, you can create multiple income streams and establish a strong personal brand.

Kai Alleyne, an ambitious software developer from Barbados, always had a passion for technology. Growing up on the island, he was fascinated by how technology could solve complex problems and bring people together. After earning a degree in computer science, Kai returned to Barbados with a strong desire to make a difference in his community. However, he soon realised that the tech scene on the island was still in its infancy, with few opportunities for growth.

Rather than feeling discouraged, Kai decided to focus on mastering a specific skill that he believed would be in high demand in the future: cybersecurity. He saw that as more businesses in the Caribbean moved online, there would be a critical need for experts who could protect digital assets and ensure the security of sensitive information.

Kai began his journey by investing heavily in continuous learning. He enrolled in advanced online courses, attended cybersecurity conferences abroad, and even found a mentor in the United States who was a seasoned cybersecurity expert. Kai dedicated countless hours to honing his skills, often staying up late to complete certifications and working on real-world projects to build his experience.

As his expertise grew, Kai started sharing his knowledge through local tech meetups, social media, and eventually by writing a blog. His insights on cybersecurity were well-received, and he quickly built a reputation as the go-to expert on the island. Local businesses began approaching him for advice, and he started offering consulting services, helping companies secure their digital infrastructure.

Kai's reputation continued to grow, and he soon realised there was an opportunity to monetise his expertise further. He developed an online course in cybersecurity specifically tailored for small businesses in the Caribbean. The course was a hit, attracting students not just from Barbados but from across the region. Kai's mastery of cybersecurity became the foundation of his business, allowing him to generate income through consulting, teaching, and digital products.

Kai's story illustrates the power of mastering a single skill and leveraging it to create multiple streams of income. By focusing deeply on cybersecurity, he was able to turn his passion into a thriving business that not only benefited him but also contributed to the growth of the tech ecosystem in the Caribbean.

Master one skill deeply, and it can open doors you never knew existed.

Key Action Points from Kai's Story

- **Identify Your Core Skill:** Like Kai, focus on an area where you have both a strong interest and the potential to excel. This specialisation can become the cornerstone of your professional success.
- **Invest in Continuous Learning:** Dedicate time and resources to becoming an expert in your chosen field. Kai's commitment to learning and his willingness to seek mentorship were key factors in his success.
- **Share Your Knowledge:** Begin sharing your expertise through platforms like social media, blogging, or speaking engagements. Kai's consistent sharing helped him build credibility and attract clients.
- **Monetise Your Skill:** Explore different ways to monetise your expertise, just as Kai did by offering consulting services and creating an online course. This approach can create diverse income streams from a single skill.

28. Harnessing Diverse Skills for Career Growth and Direction

Maximising your career potential requires leveraging all your skills, even those that seem unrelated. Rather than compartmentalising talents, integrate them to create a unique value proposition in your professional journey.

Hana Mekonnen, a creative and driven professional from Ethiopia, had always nurtured a deep passion for both technology and art. After completing her studies in computer science at Addis Ababa University, she found herself increasingly fascinated by graphic design and storytelling. Initially, Hana felt a strong pressure to choose between her technical skills and her creative talents, believing that focusing exclusively on one area would lead to a more straightforward and successful career path. However, as she ventured into the job market, she began to see that her diverse skill set could actually be her greatest asset.

Hana embarked on her professional journey as a software developer at a dynamic tech startup in Addis Ababa. Although she excelled in her role, her creative side continued to call to her. Rather than suppressing this aspect of her personality, Hana found ways to integrate her graphic design skills into her work. She began by designing visually engaging presentations and developing user-friendly interfaces that seamlessly combined functionality with aesthetic appeal. Her innovative approach did not go unnoticed; her colleagues and superiors quickly recognised the added value of her diverse talents.

This blending of skills soon set Hana apart in a competitive industry. Her unique combination of technical and creative expertise led to an exciting opportunity to lead a project focused on redesigning the company's website and mobile application. Leveraging her dual skill set, Hana created a platform that was both visually stunning and highly functional. The result was a significant boost in user engagement and customer satisfaction, which further highlighted the effectiveness of her integrated approach.

Understanding the impact of her multifaceted skills, Hana took a proactive stance towards her career development. She actively sought out projects and roles that would allow her to apply all of her abilities, rather than waiting for opportunities to arise. This proactive mindset not only accelerated her career advancement but also enhanced her job satisfaction, as she was able to fully express her talents in her work.

Hana also recognised the importance of effectively communicating her unique value to her superiors. During performance reviews and career discussions, she consistently highlighted how her combined skills had benefited the organisation. By providing specific examples, such as the success of the website redesign project, Hana demonstrated the tangible impact of her contributions. This approach not only secured her promotions but also established her reputation as a forward-thinking and innovative leader within the company.

Hana Mekonnen's journey is a testament to the power of embracing and integrating diverse skills. Her ability to merge technical proficiency with creative flair allowed her to stand out and make a significant impact in her field. By proactively seeking out opportunities and effectively communicating her value, Hana not only advanced her career but also set a powerful example of how combining distinct talents can lead to exceptional success.

You don't want to feel like you've wasted any time learning a new skill. Instead, ask yourself how you can apply this skill to the next stage of your journey.

Key Action Points from Hana's Story

- **Evaluate Your Skill Set:** Like Hana, take stock of all your abilities, including those not directly related to your current job. Consider how each skill can contribute to your overall value.
- **Integrate Skills into Your Work:** Find ways to incorporate your diverse skills into your daily tasks. Hana's integration of graphic design into her software development work allowed her to stand out and add significant value to her projects.
- **Be Proactive in Career Development:** Don't wait for opportunities to come to you. Seek out roles or projects where you can apply your full range of skills. Hana's proactive approach led to faster career advancement and greater job satisfaction.
- **Communicate Your Unique Value:** When discussing career opportunities or during performance reviews, highlight how your diverse skill set benefits the organisation. Use specific examples to demonstrate your impact, just as Hana did to secure her promotions.

29. The Power of Adaptability and Agility in Navigating Business Challenges

Adaptability is a critical skill for leaders navigating the fast-paced and unpredictable business world. By staying agile and open to change, leaders can turn challenges into opportunities, leading their teams with confidence through uncertain terrain.

In the vibrant city of Kingston, Jamaica, Akilah Davies, a young entrepreneur with roots in the Caribbean, was making waves in the eco-friendly fashion industry. Her business, Green Roots Apparel, had quickly gained attention for using sustainable materials and supporting local artisans. With her innovative designs and commitment to ethical fashion, Akilah's brand was growing fast. However, a major challenge was on the horizon.

One morning, Akilah received news that one of her largest suppliers, a small farming cooperative in Haiti, was facing difficulties due to a natural disaster. The cooperative, which provided her with organic cotton, was unable to meet its commitments for the upcoming season. This disruption posed a serious threat to Akilah's production timelines, and the pressure was mounting as she prepared for the international launch of her latest collection.

Unsure of how to proceed, Akilah reached out to a trusted business advisor, Isabella Reyes, a seasoned entrepreneur from Brazil. Isabella had faced similar disruptions in her own agricultural export business and understood the importance of adaptability in such moments. "Akilah," Isabella advised, "This is the time to be agile. You can't control everything, but you can control how you respond. Look for alternatives, even if it means pivoting your strategy."

Taking Isabella's advice to heart, Akilah gathered her team to brainstorm solutions. They discussed sourcing cotton from different suppliers, but many options did not align with Green Roots' ethical standards. Then, Akilah had an idea—why not expand the product line to include locally sourced hemp fabric, a sustainable alternative that was gaining popularity in the fashion world? With a renewed sense of purpose, Akilah quickly partnered with a nearby hemp farm in Jamaica and adjusted her designs to incorporate this new material. She reworked her marketing strategy to highlight the benefits of hemp, focusing on its durability and eco-friendliness. This pivot not only allowed Akilah to meet her production deadlines but also positioned Green Roots Apparel as an innovative leader in the sustainable fashion movement.

The international launch was a huge success. Customers praised the bold move to incorporate hemp, and media outlets highlighted Green Roots Apparel's adaptability in the face of adversity. What could have been a devastating setback turned into a breakthrough for Akilah and her brand.

Akilah's story illustrates the power of adaptability and agility in business. By staying flexible and open to new possibilities, she was able to overcome a major challenge and come out stronger on the other side. Her ability to pivot, combined with a willingness to embrace change, allowed her to lead her company through uncertain times and seize new opportunities.

Success in business often depends on our ability to adapt to unforeseen challenges and turn them into opportunities for growth.

Key Action Points from Akilah's Story

- **Be Open to Change:** When challenges arise, look for new opportunities rather than focusing on obstacles. Akilah's ability to pivot her product offering allowed her to thrive.
- **Leverage Your Network:** Akilah sought advice from Isabella, demonstrating the value of having a strong network to help guide you through difficult decisions.
- **Stay True to Your Values:** Even as Akilah adapted, she remained committed to her core values of sustainability and ethical sourcing, ensuring that her brand stayed authentic.
- **Act Quickly but Strategically:** In moments of crisis, it's important to make swift decisions, but also consider how they align with your long-term goals, as Akilah did with her marketing strategy.

30. The Confidence Equation to Lead with Certainty in Uncertain Times

In times of uncertainty, confident leadership is key. Leaders who stay composed, make decisive choices, and inspire others with their vision can navigate their teams through challenges. Confidence is not about having all the answers, but about trusting your ability to make sound decisions and adjust as needed.

In Kingston, Jamaica, Jelani Clarke, a Jamaican-American entrepreneur, had built his company, "EcoBuild Solutions," into a respected player in the sustainable construction industry. EcoBuild specialised in creating eco-friendly, hurricane resistant homes across the Caribbean, a region vulnerable to extreme weather. Jelani had always been confident in his mission and his team's expertise, but a sudden shift in the global economy left him facing unexpected challenges.

As global supply chains began to crumble due to a series of unforeseen events—ranging from pandemic restrictions to shipping delays—EcoBuild's construction materials were stuck in ports around the world. Projects stalled, and clients grew anxious. What was once a thriving business had been brought to a near halt, and Jelani's team looked to him for answers. With so much out of his control, Jelani knew this was a moment that required him to lead with calm, confidence, and clarity.

Unsure of the best path forward, Jelani sought advice from his long-time friend, Sofia Mendes, a Portuguese logistics expert who had successfully guided her own business through difficult times. Over a video call, Sofia shared her perspective: "Jelani, it's not about having all the answers right now. You won't be able to solve everything overnight. What your team and your clients need is certainty—certainty that you will lead them through this. Show confidence in the decisions you make, even as things evolve."

Sofia's words struck a chord with Jelani. He realised that while he couldn't control the external forces impacting his business, he could control how he responded. He called a company-wide meeting, acknowledging the uncertainty they were all facing but expressing his confidence in the team's ability to weather the storm. Jelani assured his employees that they would pivot, find solutions, and emerge stronger.

He immediately set his leadership team to work on contingency plans, exploring alternative suppliers and local material sources to keep projects moving. He also communicated openly with clients, providing transparent updates while reassuring them that EcoBuild remained committed to delivering their projects. Jelani's calm and decisive approach inspired trust, and though the road ahead was uncertain, his confidence helped his team stay focused and motivated.

Within months, EcoBuild had successfully restructured its supply chain, relying more on local materials and regional suppliers. While the challenges hadn't disappeared, Jelani's leadership had kept the company afloat and, in some ways, made it more resilient for the future. His confidence in leading through the uncertainty gave his team the stability they needed to keep moving forward.

Confidence in uncertain times isn't about knowing everything, it's about leading with conviction and showing others that together, you'll find a way through.

Key Action Points from Jelani's Story

- **Lead with Confidence, Even in Uncertainty:** Jelani's ability to maintain a calm, confident demeanour in the face of disruption helped keep his team focused and motivated.
- **Control What You Can:** Although Jelani couldn't solve every external problem, he focused on what he could control—pivoting to alternative suppliers and keeping communication open.
- **Inspire Trust Through Transparency:** Jelani's transparency with his team and clients created trust, even when answers weren't immediately clear.
- **Confidence Doesn't Require Certainty:** Leading with confidence isn't about having all the answers; it's about showing the ability to adapt and guiding others with decisiveness.

31. Making Bold Moves to Cultivate Courage and Lead in Uncharted Waters

Leadership in uncharted waters requires boldness and courage. Stepping into the unknown can feel risky, but leaders who embrace uncertainty with conviction and make brave decisions inspire others to follow and achieve breakthroughs that would otherwise seem impossible.

Sharesse Baptiste, a Caribbean entrepreneur with roots in St. Lucia had built her company, "Oceana Ventures," into a thriving business. Specialising in marine-based tourism and eco-conscious ocean exploration, Oceana Ventures catered to travellers seeking environmentally friendly ways to experience the beauty of the Caribbean's waters.

However, as the global economy shifted and environmental concerns grew more urgent, Sharesse faced a tough decision: should she stay the course with her traditional tourism model, or venture into the uncharted territory of sustainability-driven ocean research? Several organisations had approached her about using her fleet for scientific studies focused on coral reef restoration and ocean health, but making that pivot would mean rethinking her business model, taking financial risks, and navigating an industry she knew little about.

Feeling conflicted, Sharesse reached out to Marco Diaz, a Chilean marine biologist who had spent years studying ocean ecosystems. They met at a conference on sustainable tourism in Mexico, and over dinner, Sharesse expressed her hesitation. "I've built this company on the idea of creating unforgettable experiences for people, and now I'm being asked to take it in a whole new direction. What if I'm making the wrong move?" Marco smiled and said, "Sharesse, sometimes the greatest leaps come from the boldest moves. You've already built a company that respects the ocean. Now you have a chance to lead in its preservation, not just for tourism but for future generations. The question isn't if you can do it—it's if you have the courage to lead in uncharted waters."

Marco's words resonated deeply with Sharesse. She knew the decision would be challenging, but it also felt like the right thing to do—not only for her business but for the environment she loved. After careful consideration, Sharesse made the bold move to reposition Oceana Ventures as a dual-purpose company: offering marine tourism while partnering with research organisations to use her vessels for ocean conservation studies.

The transition wasn't easy. Sharesse had to secure new funding, retrain her staff, and build relationships in the scientific community. There were moments of doubt, especially when the first few months brought financial strain. But Sharesse's courage and determination paid off.

Soon, Oceana Ventures became known as an innovative leader in sustainable tourism, merging the excitement of ocean exploration with the responsibility of protecting marine ecosystems. The bold move not only revitalised her business but also attracted a new wave of eco-conscious travellers and global partnerships with environmental organisations.

Sharesse's willingness to lead in uncharted waters transformed Oceana Ventures into a symbol of progress, showing that bold leadership could drive both profit and positive environmental impact.

Courage isn't the absence of fear, it's the boldness to take the leap anyway.

Key Action Points from Sharesse's Story

- **Courageous Leadership Sparks Innovation:** Sharesse's bold decision to pivot her business toward sustainability allowed her to break new ground and become a leader in ecotourism.
- **Trust Your Instincts:** Sharesse trusted her values and instincts when faced with uncertainty, leading her to make the right decision for her business and the environment.
- **Bold Moves Often Involve Risk:** The shift wasn't easy, and there were financial risks, but Sharesse's commitment to her vision ultimately led to success.
- **Leadership in Uncharted Waters Requires Vision:** Sharesse's ability to see beyond the immediate challenges and focus on the long-term impact enabled her to lead with confidence.

32. The Role of Innovation in Future-Proofing Your Business

Innovation is crucial for businesses to stay relevant in a rapidly evolving marketplace. By proactively embracing new ideas and technologies, leaders can disrupt the status quo, rather than being disrupted by it.

In the bustling tech hub of Accra, Ghana, Jabari Mensah, a dynamic software engineer with a passion for fintech, had just launched his startup, "AduPay." His platform aimed to make financial services more accessible to underserved communities across West Africa, allowing users to transfer money, pay bills, and access loans through their mobile phones.

AduPay was gaining traction, particularly in rural areas where traditional banks had limited reach. However, Jabari soon faced an unexpected challenge. A global fintech giant announced plans to enter the African market, offering similar services, but with greater resources and established brand recognition. This move threatened to overshadow Jabari's growing business, potentially wiping out the progress he had made.

Recognizing the danger, Jabari reached out to his longtime friend and business mentor, Mei Lin, an entrepreneur from Singapore who had navigated similar competition in the Asian market. Mei advised him, "Jabari, if you want to survive, you need to innovate faster than the competition. Don't just play catch-up—create something that sets you apart."

With this advice, Jabari began to think deeply about what AduPay could offer that the competition could not. He gathered his team to brainstorm, focusing on the unique needs of their users. After several sessions, the team came up with a groundbreaking idea: a feature that would allow users without internet access to perform financial transactions using basic SMS technology, bypassing the need for smartphones or data plans.

Jabari and his team worked tirelessly to implement the new feature. They also partnered with local mobile network providers to offer AduPay services at reduced rates in rural areas. This move resonated deeply with their target audience, as it addressed a real gap in the market that the larger competitors had overlooked.

The innovation paid off. Not only did AduPay retain its market share, but it also expanded rapidly, attracting new users who appreciated the platform's inclusivity. Jabari's ability to disrupt the market with a unique solution positioned AduPay as a leader in fintech innovation in West Africa.

Jabari's story shows the importance of staying ahead of the curve through innovation. By embracing new ideas and listening to the needs of his customers, he was able to future-proof his business and thrive in a highly competitive environment.

Innovation is not just about creating something new—it's about solving problems in ways that matter to the people who need it most.

Key Action Points from Jabri's Story

- **Innovate Before You're Forced To:** By proactively seeking out innovative solutions, Jabari was able to disrupt the market instead of being disrupted.
- **Listen to Your Customers:** Jabari's success came from understanding the specific needs of his users, particularly those in rural areas, and tailoring his solution accordingly.
- **Leverage Strategic Partnerships:** Partnering with local mobile networks allowed AduPay to offer services at a reduced cost, providing additional value to customers.
- **Stay Agile and Adapt:** Jabari's willingness to pivot and implement new technology set him apart from larger competitors, showing the value of flexibility in business.

33. Building Teams that Bring Their A-Game Every Day

Attracting and retaining top talent isn't just about competitive salaries or perks; it's about creating an environment where people feel valued, challenged, and motivated. Leaders who foster a culture of growth, innovation, and support can build teams that consistently perform at their best.

Zola Mphahlele, a South African-Canadian entrepreneur, founded "HealthWave," a telemedicine platform designed to make healthcare accessible to remote communities. The company's mission was clear, but as HealthWave expanded, Zola struggled to build a team that could keep up with the company's rapid growth while maintaining high standards of innovation and care.

Although she had hired skilled professionals, Zola noticed that her team lacked the motivation and cohesion needed to push HealthWave to the next level. The company had the talent, but they weren't consistently bringing their A-game. Realising that something needed to change, Zola reached out to her former colleague, Maria Torres, an ArgentiNalan organisational psychologist working in New York. Maria had a reputation for helping companies develop high-performing teams.

Maria's advice was simple but powerful: "Zola, people are drawn to environments where they feel challenged and supported. If you want your team to bring their best every day, you need to create a culture that fosters growth, collaboration, and a sense of purpose."

Taking Maria's words to heart, Zola revamped HealthWave's approach to talent. She started by creating opportunities for professional development, including mentorship programs and skill-building workshops, so employees could continuously learn and grow. She also implemented a more collaborative approach to innovation, encouraging team members to contribute ideas and take ownership of new projects.

Zola made sure to recognize and celebrate achievements, creating a system that highlighted individual and team successes. Most importantly, she fostered a culture where the company's mission—improving healthcare access—was front and centre, giving her team a clear sense of purpose that motivated them to excel.

As a result, HealthWave's team transformed into a high-performing unit, with each member bringing their best to work every day. Employees became more engaged, innovation flourished, and HealthWave's reputation as a leader in telemedicine grew rapidly. Zola's leadership, focused on creating a culture of talent magnetism, turned her team into one that consistently exceeded expectations.

When people feel valued, challenged, and connected to a purpose, they'll bring their best every day.

Key Action Points from Zola's Story

- **Foster Growth and Development:** By offering continuous learning opportunities, Zola ensured her team felt challenged and engaged, helping them bring their best to work.
- **Encourage Collaboration and Ownership:** Zola's collaborative approach to innovation empowered her team, fostering creativity and accountability.
- **Recognize and Celebrate Success:** Regularly acknowledging both individual and team accomplishments motivated employees to strive for excellence.
- **Connect the Team to a Purpose:** Zola's focus on HealthWave's mission gave her team a strong sense of purpose, driving motivation and commitment to their work.

34. Embracing Failure as Fuel and Turning Setbacks into Springboards for Success

Failure is not a final destination but a necessary step on the path to success. By learning from setbacks and applying those lessons, entrepreneurs can turn failure into a powerful catalyst for growth and innovation.

In the city of Paris, France, Malika Diouf, a Senegalese-French fashion designer, had always dreamed of launching her own fashion line. Known for her bold designs that blended modern European chic with traditional West African patterns, Malika had been working for years in the Paris fashion industry, gaining valuable experience. Her moment finally came when she launched her brand, "Diouf Couture."

At first, her brand received positive reviews, and her designs were featured in several small fashion shows. Emboldened by the initial buzz, Malika decided to take a big risk by debuting her new collection at Paris Fashion Week. She invested everything into the launch—financially, emotionally, and creatively. But when her show day arrived, it didn't go as planned. The collection didn't resonate with the audience, and critics were harsh, calling it "incohesive" and "underwhelming." Devastated, Malika felt like she had failed on the most important stage of her career.

Unsure of what to do next, Malika sought the advice of her friend and mentor, Sophie Patel, an Indian-British designer who had experienced similar struggles early in her career. "Malika," Sophie said, "I know this feels like the end, but it's just the beginning. Failure doesn't define you; how you respond does. Look at what went wrong, learn from it, and come back stronger."

With Sophie's words in mind, Malika took time to reflect on what went wrong. She realised that in trying to appeal to too many audiences at once, she had lost her brand's identity. She returned to her roots and spent months refining her vision, focusing on creating designs that were more authentic to her personal style and heritage.

Malika also began connecting with smaller, independent fashion platforms across Europe and Africa, showcasing her collection in intimate settings where she could build deeper connections with her audience. This shift in strategy paid off. Her rebranded designs were embraced by a niche but loyal following, and her work gained attention for its bold fusion of cultures. Within two years, Diouf Couture became a respected name in the industry, known for its authenticity and innovation.

Malika's setback at Paris Fashion Week was not the end of her journey but the fuel she needed to refine her brand and achieve lasting success.

Failure doesn't mean you're finished. It's the universe pushing you to find a better way, a more authentic path to success.

Key Action Points from Malika's Story

- **Failure Can Refine Your Vision:** Malika's initial failure helped her realise that her brand needed to be more focused and authentic. It allowed her to refine her approach and stay true to her identity.
- **Seek Advice from Those Who Have Been There:** Malika's mentor, Sophie, provided guidance and perspective, showing the value of learning from others who have faced similar challenges.
- **Success Comes in Phases:** While Paris Fashion Week wasn't the breakthrough Malika hoped for, it opened the door to smaller opportunities that eventually led to larger success.
- **Persistence is Key:** By not giving up after her initial failure, Malika transformed her brand into something stronger, proving that perseverance is essential in the face of setbacks.

35. Leading with Vision and Crafting a Strategy That Speaks to the Future

A clear and forward-thinking vision is crucial for long-term success in business. By crafting a strategy that not only addresses current challenges but also anticipates future trends, leaders can guide their businesses toward sustainable growth.

In London, Adrian Gooding, a Black British entrepreneur with roots in Barbados, had built a successful business called "FutureSound," a tech company focused on creating AI-powered music tools for aspiring musicians. His products had revolutionised how artists could compose, produce, and distribute their music, making advanced technology accessible to all.

FutureSound was flourishing, but as new competitors entered the market and technology continued to evolve, Adrian knew he needed a long-term strategy to maintain his company's competitive edge. He wanted to do more than just react to current trends—he wanted to lead them.

Unsure of the best path forward, Adrian reached out to his business partner and friend, Haruto Takahashi, a Japanese-American tech entrepreneur who had successfully scaled his own company in Silicon Valley. Haruto shared his experiences with Adrian, emphasising the importance of a strong vision. "Adrian," Haruto said, "Don't just think about where the industry is today—think about where it's going. What does the future of music look like, and how can FutureSound be at the centre of it?"

Inspired by Haruto's advice, Adrian began to focus on long-term strategic planning. He analysed emerging technologies, such as virtual reality and blockchain, and explored how they might intersect with the music industry. After months of research and collaboration with his team, Adrian unveiled a new vision for FutureSound: a platform that would allow artists to create immersive, interactive music experiences in virtual worlds, leveraging AI and blockchain to ensure that creators could retain full ownership of their work.

Adrian's vision wasn't just about keeping up with technology; it was about pioneering a new way for people to experience music. His strategy included partnering with VR companies and blockchain developers, ensuring that FutureSound would be at the forefront of this emerging trend. By focusing on where the industry was headed, rather than where it currently stood, Adrian positioned his company as a visionary leader in music technology.

Over time, FutureSound became synonymous with innovation in the music space, attracting top artists and earning recognition for its forward-thinking approach. Adrian's vision not only kept the company relevant but also set the stage for long-term growth.

True leadership is about seeing beyond the present and crafting a future that others can't yet imagine.

Key Action Points from Adrian's Story

- **Think Long-Term:** Adrian's success came from looking beyond current trends and anticipating where the industry was heading, allowing him to craft a forward-thinking strategy.
- **Leverage Technology:** By exploring emerging technologies like VR and blockchain, Adrian positioned his company to be a leader in the next wave of innovation.
- **Collaboration is Key:** Adrian's partnership with Haruto and his team was essential in shaping his vision, showing the importance of seeking advice and diverse perspectives.
- **Be a Pioneer, Not a Follower:** Instead of reacting to competitors, Adrian led with a bold new vision for the future of music, allowing him to define the direction of his industry.

36. The Power of Quiet Leadership to Inspire Through Action, Not Words

Quiet leadership is about influencing others through consistent action, integrity, and example rather than grand speeches or bold declarations. True leaders inspire those around them by showing what is possible through their work and dedication.

Amara Jatta, a soft-spoken entrepreneur of Gambian descent living in Johannesburg, ran a successful social enterprise called "EcoRevive." Her company specialised in converting waste materials into affordable, eco-friendly building materials, helping to address both housing shortages and environmental challenges in the region.

While Amara wasn't known for delivering rousing speeches or dominating boardroom discussions, her quiet determination and relentless focus on the company's mission had earned her deep respect among her team and in the community. Under her leadership, EcoRevive had grown steadily, providing employment to hundreds of locals while also making a positive environmental impact.

One day, Amara's business hit a major roadblock. A crucial investor unexpectedly pulled out of a project that was set to expand EcoRevive's operations into neighbouring countries. The team was disheartened, and many wondered whether the company could continue without the much-needed capital infusion.

Amara didn't react with frustration or loud motivational speeches. Instead, she calmly gathered her team and quietly went back to work. She spent long hours researching alternative funding options, and soon, her actions began to inspire those around her. Amara's steadfastness in the face of adversity ignited a renewed sense of commitment in her team.

A few weeks later, without much fanfare, Amara announced that she had secured a partnership with a local government agency focused on sustainable development. The deal provided not only the funds needed to move forward but also long-term support for EcoRevive's growth. Amara's quiet resilience had turned the company's challenges into opportunities, all without raising her voice.

Her team admired her more than ever, not for what she said, but for what she did. Amara's leadership style—marked by action and consistency—had created a culture of perseverance and integrity that others naturally wanted to follow.

Leadership isn't about being the loudest in the room. It's about quietly doing the right thing, even when no one is watching.

Key Action Points from Amara's Story

- **Lead by Example:** Amara's quiet leadership proved that consistent actions often speak louder than words. Her dedication inspired her team more effectively than any speech.
- **Stay Calm in Crisis:** Amara's composed approach in the face of challenges allowed her to think clearly and guide her company through difficult times.
- **Inspire Through Integrity:** By staying true to her values and mission, Amara earned the trust and loyalty of her team and community.
- **Quiet Leadership is Powerful:** Amara demonstrated that leadership doesn't always need to be loud; sometimes, the most effective leaders inspire by doing rather than talking.

37. From Ideas to Execution to Bridge the Gap with Strategic Clarity

Turning great ideas into successful outcomes requires strategic clarity. Without a clear roadmap, even the best ideas can falter. Effective execution depends on defining goals, identifying the right resources, and maintaining focus on key priorities.

In the lively city of Accra, Ghana, Kojo Agyeman, a Ghanaian-American entrepreneur, founded "SolarWays," a renewable energy company with the goal of bringing affordable solar energy solutions to rural communities in West Africa. Kojo was passionate about sustainability and had a grand vision to make SolarWays a leading force in renewable energy on the continent.

However, despite his ambitious ideas, SolarWays struggled to gain traction. Kojo's team worked hard on innovative products, but their efforts were scattered, and progress was slow. The company was burning through resources without making significant headway in their mission.

Feeling frustrated, Kojo reached out to his friend, Lucia Ferreira, a Brazilian strategy consultant based in São Paulo, for guidance. Lucia quickly saw that the problem wasn't Kojo's vision—it was the lack of strategic clarity. She asked Kojo to take a step back and clearly define the company's goals. "Kojo, your ideas are great, but without a clear strategy, they're just ideas. Let's break it down."

Together, Kojo and Lucia identified three key priorities for SolarWays: 1) focus on one flagship solar product, 2) secure funding for a pilot project, and 3) build partnerships with local governments and NGOs to expand access to the technology. By narrowing down the scope of the business and developing a strategic roadmap, Kojo finally had a clear path forward.

With this newfound clarity, Kojo led his team to focus on a portable solar generator specifically designed for rural households. They secured funding from an international development organization and launched a pilot project in a village in Northern Ghana. The pilot was a success, and with the data collected, SolarWays was able to prove the viability of their product and secure more funding to expand into other regions.

Within two years, SolarWays became a recognised name in West Africa's renewable energy sector. Kojo's leadership and strategic clarity allowed the company to execute effectively, turning SolarWays into a business that not only had a vision but also delivered real impact.

A great idea is only the beginning. It's the clarity of your strategy that brings it to life and transforms vision into reality.

Key Action Points from Kojo's Story

- **Strategic Clarity Turns Ideas into Action:** Kojo's success came when he developed a clear roadmap, turning his big ideas into actionable steps.
- **Prioritise and Focus:** Instead of trying to tackle everything at once, Kojo narrowed down SolarWays' goals, leading to more focused and effective execution.
- **Use Pilot Projects to Prove Concepts:** By testing their product on a smaller scale, SolarWays was able to gather data and build credibility, making it easier to scale later.
- **Collaborate with Strategic Partners:** Kojo's partnerships with local governments and NGOs played a crucial role in expanding SolarWays' impact and reaching more communities.

38. Daring to be Different and the Competitive Advantage of Diversity in Thought

In today's global business environment, embracing diversity of thought fosters innovation and creates a competitive advantage. Different perspectives drive creativity, uncover untapped markets, and lead to better problem-solving.

Zuri Achieng, a Kenyan entrepreneur with Luo roots, was the founder of "TechWeave," a tech company specialising in AI-powered education platforms for under-resourced schools in East Africa. Zuri's goal was to close the education gap for students who lacked access to modern learning tools. But the challenge was immense—global giants in ed-tech were expanding into Africa, and her small team of engineers struggled to keep up with the pace of development and the vast financial resources of larger competitors.

Feeling the pressure to innovate, Zuri decided to approach the problem differently. She reached out to her long-time collaborator, Ravi Patel, an Indian software engineer based in Mumbai, India. Ravi brought with him an entirely different approach to problem-solving, shaped by his work on AI tools for rural education in India. Together, they brainstormed ideas, combining Zuri's deep understanding of the unique challenges facing African schools with Ravi's technical expertise in scalable digital solutions.

Ravi introduced Zuri to a concept that was widely used in India: community-based learning through mobile devices. While many companies were focused on building complex platforms that required high-speed internet and advanced hardware, Ravi suggested that they design an offline-first model—one that would run on basic smartphones and work even in areas with limited internet connectivity.

Inspired by Ravi's perspective, Zuri and her team revamped their platform. They developed a mobile-first AI tutor that could work offline and support local languages, making it accessible to students in rural areas without high-speed internet. The AI tutor was designed to be adaptive, meaning it could tailor lessons to each student's learning pace and needs, creating a more personalised education experience.

Their new product was an instant hit. Schools across Kenya and neighbouring countries quickly adopted TechWeave's solution, as it provided a practical and affordable tool to improve learning outcomes. Zuri's willingness to integrate diverse perspectives not only gave her company an edge over competitors but also opened doors to partnerships with education ministries across East Africa.

Within two years, TechWeave expanded its reach to more than 15 countries in Africa, helping over 500,000 students access quality education. The diversity of thought between Zuri and Ravi was the driving force behind the innovation that allowed TechWeave to stand out in a crowded market.

True innovation comes from diversity of thought. When you open your mind to perspectives beyond your own, you open doors to endless possibilities.

Key Action Points from Zuri's Story

- **Diversity of Thought Drives Innovation:** Zuri's collaboration with Ravi allowed TechWeave to tap into new ideas and solutions, driving innovation that solved a critical problem for their market.
- **Cross-Cultural Collaboration is a Competitive Advantage:** By combining insights from different cultural and business environments, Zuri was able to create a product that met the specific needs of her target audience.
- **Local Context Matters:** Zuri's deep understanding of the unique challenges in East African schools gave her an edge, but it was the integration of diverse perspectives that pushed TechWeave's solution beyond expectations.
- **Adapt to the Market, Don't Follow It:** Instead of trying to keep up with global ed-tech companies, Zuri adapted her product to meet the specific needs of her market, making her business more resilient and competitive.

39. Seizing Opportunities you Didn't Plan for in Business

Sometimes, the greatest opportunities arise unexpectedly. Being open to these moments of strategic serendipity and having the agility to adapt can lead to breakthroughs that propel your business forward.

Mae Akuffo, a British-Ghanaian business consultant, ran a small firm called "Elevate" that specialised in helping startups streamline their operations. Her clientele mostly consisted of small tech companies and local entrepreneurs. Although her business was doing well, Mae had always dreamt of expanding into international markets but didn't know how or where to begin.

One rainy afternoon, Mae was at a networking event when she met Li Wei, a Chinese-American venture capitalist based in Hong Kong. They struck up a casual conversation about the global tech industry and the challenges startups face when scaling. Li was intrigued by Mae's approach to business consulting and how she focused on creating customised solutions rather than using a one-size-fits-all model.

A few weeks later, Li contacted Mae out of the blue with a proposition. He was investing in several startups across Southeast Asia and believed they could benefit from her expertise. Li offered to introduce Mae to these companies and suggested she travel to Hong Kong to meet with potential clients. It was an opportunity that Mae hadn't planned for, but she was intrigued.

Despite the risks and uncertainty, Mae seized the moment. She flew to Hong Kong, where she not only met with Li's portfolio companies but also connected with other investors and entrepreneurs in the region. During her meetings, Mae quickly realised that many startups in Asia faced similar operational challenges as those in the UK, but they lacked access to tailored consulting services like hers.

Her visit led to several new contracts, and within six months, Mae had opened a satellite office in Hong Kong. This expansion brought in major clients from across Southeast Asia, dramatically growing her business beyond what she had initially envisioned. What began as a chance encounter at a networking event turned into a strategic pivot that transformed Elevate into an international consulting firm.

Mae's success was a direct result of her ability to recognise an unexpected opportunity and move quickly to capitalise on it. By staying open to serendipity, she positioned her business for growth in a way she had never anticipated.

Opportunity often comes disguised as a chance encounter and your willingness to act on the unexpected that can take your business to places you never imagined.

Key Action Points from Mae's Story

- **Be Open to the Unexpected:** Mae's willingness to engage in a casual conversation led to a life-changing opportunity. Sometimes, the most significant opportunities come when you're not looking for them.
- **Move Quickly When Opportunity Knocks:** Once the opportunity presented itself, Mae didn't hesitate. Her quick action allowed her to take full advantage of an unexpected opening.
- **Think Beyond Borders:** By stepping out of her comfort zone and exploring international markets, Mae expanded her business in ways she hadn't originally planned.
- **Build Relationships, Not Just Transactions:** Mae's relationship with Li Wei wasn't just about business. Their mutual respect and shared interest led to a partnership that benefited both sides.

40. Breaking Through the Noise and Standing Out in a Saturated Market

In a crowded marketplace, differentiation is key. By staying true to your unique vision and focusing on what makes your business distinct, you can break through the noise and capture attention, even in the most competitive industries.

In the dynamic city of Toronto, Canada, Kofi Badu, an African-Canadian entrepreneur with roots in Ghana, had just launched his startup, "Badu Coffee." His vision was simple yet ambitious: to bring the rich flavours of single-origin West African coffee to the global stage. However, the coffee market was already saturated with countless brands, from massive international chains to artisanal local roasters.

Kofi quickly realised that breaking through the noise would be his biggest challenge. Despite having an excellent product, Badu Coffee struggled to stand out among the sea of competitors, and sales were slow. To make matters worse, major coffee brands were dominating the market with massive advertising budgets, something Kofi simply couldn't match.

Feeling the pressure, Kofi turned to his friend, Elena Gonzalez, a marketing strategist from Spain, for advice. Elena, known for her creative approach, offered a fresh perspective. "Kofi, in a market this crowded, you can't outspend the competition, but you can outsmart them. Focus on what makes Badu Coffee unique—your story, your culture, and the direct relationships you have with the farmers in Ghana. Lean into what no one else can offer."

Inspired by Elena's words, Kofi shifted his strategy. Instead of trying to compete head-on with larger brands, he leaned into his unique selling proposition: Badu Coffee wasn't just another artisanal brand, it was a direct link between West African coffee farmers and consumers. He rebranded his product to highlight its cultural heritage, telling the stories of the farmers who grew the beans and emphasising the ethical, direct trade relationships he had built.

Kofi also focused on creating a personal connection with his audience. He hosted "Coffee Conversations" at local cafes, where customers could taste his coffee while learning about the origins of the beans and the communities that produced them. His authenticity resonated with customers who wanted more than just a good cup of coffee—they wanted to support a meaningful cause.

Badu Coffee's unique positioning quickly attracted attention. Media outlets began featuring Kofi's story, and customers who were passionate about sustainability and ethical sourcing became loyal brand advocates. What started as a struggling startup became a beloved brand with a loyal following, standing out in a highly competitive market through its authenticity and cultural roots.

In a crowded market, your greatest asset is your authenticity. Stand firm in your story, and the right people will listen.

Key Action Points from Kofi's Story

- **Embrace Your Unique Story:** Kofi's success came when he focused on what made his brand unique—his direct connection to Ghanaian coffee farmers and his cultural heritage.
- **Compete with Authenticity, Not Budgets:** Kofi couldn't compete with the advertising budgets of large companies, so he focused on building genuine connections with his customers.
- **Leverage Niche Marketing:** By hosting intimate events and sharing his brand's story, Kofi created a loyal customer base that valued both the product and the mission behind it.
- **Cultural Authenticity Matters:** By embracing his roots and telling the story of West African coffee, Kofi tapped into a growing market for ethically sourced and culturally significant products.

41. Scaling with Intention and Avoiding Growth for Growth's Sake

Sustainable growth is intentional and aligned with long-term vision. Growing too fast without strategy can lead to inefficiencies, loss of culture, and a diluted brand. Scaling with purpose ensures that expansion enhances rather than undermines your core values and mission.

Imani Dembélé, a French-Ivorian entrepreneur, founded "Éclat Naturel," a luxury skincare brand that focused on organic ingredients sourced from West Africa. Imani's passion was rooted in her heritage—she used shea butter and other natural ingredients harvested from small communities in Côte d'Ivoire. Her brand quickly gained popularity in France, known for its high-quality products and ethical sourcing practices.

As Éclat Naturel grew in popularity, larger retailers across Europe and the United States began to approach Imani with lucrative distribution deals. The prospect of expanding into these international markets was tempting, but Imani hesitated. The rapid growth could easily outpace her production capabilities, and scaling too fast risked compromising her brand's core values—quality, sustainability, and community partnership.

Feeling the pressure to expand, Imani sought advice from her mentor, Anaïs Rodriguez, a Spanish businesswoman who had successfully scaled her own ethical fashion brand. Anaïs cautioned Imani about the dangers of growing too quickly. "Imani," she said, "growth isn't just about numbers; it's about doing it in a way that protects your mission. Don't lose sight of what makes Éclat Naturel special."

After reflecting on Anaïs' advice, Imani decided to take a more intentional approach to scaling. Instead of rushing into every new market opportunity, she focused on strengthening her supply chain. She worked closely with her suppliers in Côte d'Ivoire to ensure they could sustainably increase production without overexploiting resources or compromising quality. She also invested in training for the women in the cooperatives she partnered with, helping them improve their production techniques and business acumen.

Imani limited her expansion to select markets where she knew she could maintain her brand's integrity. She chose retailers who aligned with her values and were willing to promote Éclat Naturel's story of sustainability and ethical sourcing. This intentional approach allowed Imani to grow her business steadily while staying true to her mission.

Within three years, Éclat Naturel expanded to the United States, but on Imani's terms. By scaling with intention, she not only preserved the brand's reputation but also strengthened its relationship with the communities that supplied her ingredients. Her careful planning led to sustained, manageable growth, ensuring the long-term success of her business.

Growth should never come at the cost of your values. Scale with purpose, and your business will thrive for the long term.

Key Action Points from Imani's Story

- **Prioritise Values Over Rapid Growth:** Imani's success came from staying true to her values, even when tempted by fast expansion opportunities.
- **Strengthen Infrastructure Before Scaling:** Imani focused on improving her supply chain and production processes to ensure her business could grow sustainably.
- **Select Partnerships Wisely:** By partnering with retailers that shared her brand's values, Imani ensured that her company expanded in a way that aligned with its mission.
- **Intentional Growth Creates Longevity:** Imani's purposeful approach to scaling allowed her to build a strong, sustainable business without sacrificing quality or her core principles.

42. The Power of Purpose-Driven Leadership to Align Profit with Impact

Purpose-driven leadership not only drives profitability but also creates lasting impact. By aligning business objectives with meaningful societal contributions, leaders can foster deeper connections with their stakeholders, inspire their teams, and build a brand that people care about.

Malik Johnson, a Caribbean entrepreneur with a background in environmental science, founded "EcoRoots," a sustainable packaging company. Malik had always been passionate about protecting the environment and wanted his business to address the problem of plastic waste in Jamaica, where pollution from single-use plastics had become a serious issue. EcoRoots created biodegradable packaging for local food and beverage businesses, but Malik knew that if he wanted to make a real difference, he needed to scale his operations.

EcoRoots grew steadily, and Malik soon caught the attention of Mei Tanaka, a Japanese-American venture philanthropist visiting Jamaica. Mei had a keen interest in environmental initiatives and was particularly drawn to companies that aligned profit with purpose. After a few meetings, Mei proposed an investment deal that would help Malik expand EcoRoots, but she had one condition: the company's mission to reduce plastic waste had to remain at the core of its operations, no matter how large it grew.

Malik agreed, and with Mei's backing, EcoRoots began to expand across the Caribbean. However, as the company grew, Malik faced increasing pressure to prioritise profit over purpose. Large international corporations offered to buy EcoRoots' technology for a substantial sum, but they wanted to use it in ways that compromised the company's mission, such as incorporating non-sustainable materials to reduce costs.

Despite the temptation, Malik stood firm. He realised that EcoRoots' success wasn't just about making money—it was about leading with purpose and staying true to his original mission. He turned down the offers and doubled down on EcoRoots' commitment to environmental sustainability. Malik shifted his focus to developing partnerships with Caribbean governments and NGOs to tackle the region's plastic waste problem at a systemic level.

By aligning EcoRoots' goals with broader societal impact, Malik's leadership inspired a wave of environmental awareness across the region. His story was picked up by international media, and EcoRoots attracted more investment from mission-aligned partners who valued the company's purpose as much as its profit potential. EcoRoots became a symbol of how businesses could drive change while thriving financially.

Through his purpose-driven leadership, Malik not only grew EcoRoots into a profitable company but also created a legacy of environmental stewardship that resonated far beyond his initial business vision.

True leadership isn't about choosing between profit and purpose; it's about finding the balance where both can thrive.

Key Action Points from Malik's Story

- **Lead with Purpose:** Malik's decision to keep EcoRoots' mission at the core of the business allowed him to create both profit and long-term societal impact.
- **Stay True to Your Mission:** Despite pressure to compromise for financial gain, Malik remained committed to EcoRoots' sustainability goals, ensuring the company's integrity.
- **Purpose Attracts Like-Minded Partners:** By aligning his business with a meaningful purpose, Malik attracted investors and partners who shared his values and supported his vision.
- **Impact Amplifies Profit:** Malik's focus on creating positive environmental change not only grew his business but also enhanced its reputation, leading to global recognition and success.

43. Mastering the Pivot and Knowing When and How to Change Direction

In business, knowing when to pivot can be the difference between failure and success. A successful pivot requires the ability to recognise when a strategy is no longer working, and the courage to shift direction quickly while maintaining a clear vision of long-term goals.

In Amsterdam, Ayana Mbeki, a South African entrepreneur, founded "GreenCycle," a startup aimed at creating eco-friendly bicycles made from recycled materials. Ayana had always been passionate about sustainability and cycling culture, which made the concept of GreenCycle seem like the perfect business idea. Her bikes were beautifully designed and fully sustainable, but after a year of operations, sales were stagnant.

Despite a strong initial buzz, Ayana quickly realised that her eco-friendly bikes were too expensive for most consumers. The market for premium, sustainable bikes was much smaller than she had anticipated. Feeling stuck, Ayana turned to her friend, Hiroshi Sato, a Japanese entrepreneur and product designer based in Tokyo, for advice. Hiroshi had experience pivoting his own startup and encouraged Ayana to look closely at the market trends and customer feedback.

"Ayana, the idea behind GreenCycle is brilliant," Hiroshi said, "but maybe the market you're targeting is too niche. Look at what's working and what's not—there might be a better direction to take." Hiroshi's words resonated with Ayana, and she decided to pivot.

After analysing the data, Ayana noticed a growing demand for affordable, sustainable urban transport solutions, especially in cities with high traffic and pollution like Amsterdam. Instead of targeting high-end consumers, she refocused GreenCycle on creating low-cost, durable bikes made from recycled materials. The new bikes were designed for commuters and students—people who needed practical, affordable transportation with a sustainable edge.

The pivot was a turning point. Ayana partnered with universities and local governments to promote GreenCycle as part of urban sustainability programs. Within a year, GreenCycle's new, affordable model became a hit, especially among younger, environmentally conscious customers. Sales skyrocketed, and GreenCycle expanded beyond the Netherlands into several European cities.

By mastering the pivot, Ayana transformed a struggling niche product into a scalable business that aligned with the needs of her target market. GreenCycle not only survived but thrived by embracing a new direction.

A successful pivot isn't about abandoning your vision—it's about finding a new path that leads you closer to your goals while adapting to the changing market.

Key Action Points from Ayana's Story

- **Recognise When a Pivot is Needed:** Ayana's initial strategy wasn't working, and she made the crucial decision to pivot based on market feedback and trends.
- **Adapt to Market Needs:** Ayana's pivot was successful because she shifted her focus to a more relevant and scalable market—affordable urban transportation.
- **Stay True to Core Values:** Even though Ayana changed her business strategy, she stayed committed to sustainability, which remained the core of GreenCycle's identity.
- **Leverage Partnerships for Growth:** By partnering with universities and local governments, Ayana was able to scale GreenCycle quickly and reach a larger audience.

44. Future-Proofing Your Leadership and Staying Ahead of Industry Disruption

In a rapidly changing business environment, future-proofing your leadership means staying agile, continuously learning, and anticipating disruptions before they happen. Leaders who embrace innovation and proactively adjust their strategies can maintain relevance and drive long-term success.

Jelani Diop, a Senegalese tech entrepreneur, founded "AgriFlow," a startup that used AI to help farmers optimise their crop yields. Jelani's innovative platform provided data-driven insights, helping farmers in West Africa improve their productivity and profitability. As AgriFlow grew, it attracted significant attention from investors and government agencies alike.

However, just as AgriFlow began expanding into new markets, Jelani noticed a wave of technological disruption on the horizon. Major tech players were entering the agricultural sector, bringing with them advanced automation technologies that could potentially outpace his AI-based platform. Concerned about AgriFlow's long-term viability, Jelani realised that to stay ahead of this disruption, he needed to future-proof both his leadership and his company.

Jelani reached out to Lina Zhang, a Chinese-American AI specialist based in San Francisco, for guidance. Lina had vast experience in leading innovation in rapidly changing industries. She advised Jelani to embrace emerging technologies and think beyond the current scope of AgriFlow's platform. "Jelani, disruption is inevitable," she said. "But the leaders who thrive are the ones who see it coming and evolve before their competitors do."

Inspired by Lina's advice, Jelani took several steps to future-proof AgriFlow. He invested in research and development to incorporate automation and blockchain technology into the platform, making it more adaptable and scalable for farmers as technology evolved. He also formed strategic partnerships with tech giants, ensuring AgriFlow had access to the latest advancements in agricultural technology. At the same time, Jelani committed to upskilling his team, encouraging a culture of continuous learning and innovation.

By staying ahead of the curve, Jelani positioned AgriFlow as a leader in the agricultural technology space. The company not only survived the wave of disruption but thrived by offering a more comprehensive and forward-looking platform. As the industry continued to evolve, AgriFlow was well-positioned to maintain its relevance and leadership in the market.

> *The leaders who stay ahead of disruption are the ones who embrace innovation and invest in the future.*

Key Action Points from Jelani's Story

- **Anticipate Disruption:** Jelani recognised the early signs of disruption and proactively adjusted his strategy, allowing AgriFlow to stay ahead of the competition.
- **Invest in Innovation:** By investing in new technologies and research, Jelani future-proofed AgriFlow, ensuring it could evolve with industry changes.
- **Form Strategic Partnerships:** Jelani's partnerships with larger tech companies helped AgriFlow stay at the cutting edge of agricultural technology.
- **Cultivate Continuous Learning:** Jelani emphasised upskilling and innovation within his team, ensuring they were prepared to adapt to new challenges and opportunities.

45. The Invisible Force of Culture as a Strategic Asset

Company culture is an invisible yet powerful force that can drive performance, attract top talent, and create a lasting competitive advantage. When leaders prioritise culture as a strategic asset, they foster alignment, engagement, and resilience within their organisations.

Nala Aguta, a Nigerian entrepreneur, founded "InnoTech," a software company specialising in financial technology solutions for African markets. InnoTech quickly gained a reputation for its innovative products, but as the company grew, Nala realised that maintaining the vibrant, collaborative culture that had made her team so successful was becoming increasingly difficult.

As the company expanded across different regions, including East and West Africa, Nala began to see signs of misalignment. Teams in different offices struggled to collaborate effectively, and the company's fast-paced growth led to a focus on short-term results rather than the innovative, inclusive culture that had been InnoTech's hallmark. Nala knew that if she didn't address the cultural challenges, her company's growth could stall.

Nala sought advice from her mentor, Carlos Mendez, a Mexican executive who had successfully scaled his own multinational company while preserving its culture. Carlos shared his experience with Nala: "Culture is not just about ping-pong tables and fun activities. It's about the values, the way people feel connected to the mission, and how they work together. Make your culture the foundation of your strategy, and the results will follow."

Inspired by Carlos, Nala embarked on a mission to realign her company's culture with its growth strategy. She started by clearly defining InnoTech's core values—innovation, collaboration, and inclusion—and communicated them across all levels of the company. She created a leadership program that encouraged managers to embody these values and foster a sense of community across all regions.

Nala also introduced initiatives that promoted cross-team collaboration, such as monthly "Innovation Days" where employees from different regions could come together, share ideas, and work on new projects. Additionally, she implemented a recognition program to celebrate employees who exemplified InnoTech's cultural values, ensuring that culture was at the heart of everything they did.

As a result, InnoTech's culture became a key driver of its continued success. The company's alignment around its core values strengthened employee engagement, improved collaboration, and attracted top talent across the continent. By seeing culture as a strategic asset, Nala transformed her company into one where innovation and collaboration thrived, even as it scaled.

Culture isn't just a buzzword—it's the glue that holds your company together.

Key Action Points from Nala's Story

- **Culture Drives Performance:** Nala's focus on culture helped align her team's efforts, improving both innovation and collaboration across different regions.
- **Define and Communicate Core Values:** Clearly defining and reinforcing core values helped Nala create a unified culture that transcended geographical boundaries.
- **Foster Collaboration Across Teams:** By encouraging cross-regional collaboration, Nala ensured that her company maintained its innovative edge and sense of community as it grew.
- **Recognise and Celebrate Cultural Champions:** Nala's recognition program reinforced the importance of culture, motivating employees to live the company's values in their daily work.

46. Building Bridges, Not Walls in Cross-Industry Collaboration

Cross-industry collaboration is a powerful tool for fostering innovation and growth. By partnering with organisations from different sectors, businesses can tap into new ideas, broaden their reach, and create unique solutions to complex challenges.

In the heart of Johannesburg, South Africa, Zola Ndlovu, a dynamic businesswoman with Zimbabwean heritage, had made a name for herself in the renewable energy sector. Her company, SunStream Technologies, was dedicated to providing affordable solar energy solutions to underserved rural communities across Southern Africa. However, as her business grew, Zola realised that there was an untapped market she had yet to reach: urban areas. Many households in Johannesburg and other cities were still heavily reliant on fossil fuels, creating a growing demand for greener alternatives.

Despite SunStream's rural success, Zola was unsure how to position her products to appeal to urban consumers, who had more choices and different needs. She knew she needed to innovate, but she also realised that she couldn't do it alone. That's when she connected with a potential collaborator—Rajesh Patel, an up-and-coming real estate developer from India who was expanding his business into the African market. Rajesh's company, UrbanNest Properties, specialised in constructing affordable, eco-friendly housing complexes in growing cities like Johannesburg.

One afternoon, Zola and Rajesh met to discuss the possibility of collaborating. Over lunch at a busy café in Sandton, Rajesh shared his vision for building smart, sustainable housing communities that integrated renewable energy directly into the design. He was convinced that SunStream's solar technology could be a perfect fit for his projects.

"Zola," Rajesh said, "Our goals align. If we combine your energy solutions with our housing developments, we could offer a complete package—homes that are not only affordable but also energy-efficient from day one. Together, we could set a new standard for green living in urban Africa."

Intrigued by the idea, Zola saw this as the perfect opportunity to break into the urban market while staying true to her mission of sustainability. The partnership would allow her to access Rajesh's extensive network of property investors and developers, providing SunStream with the visibility and credibility it needed in the competitive city landscape.

After months of collaboration, the first UrbanNest-SunStream housing complex was unveiled in a Johannesburg suburb. The homes were equipped with cutting-edge solar panels and battery storage systems, reducing energy costs for residents and minimising the environmental footprint. The project received widespread acclaim, with both companies gaining media attention for their innovative approach to sustainable living.

The success of this cross-industry collaboration not only allowed Zola to expand her business but also introduced a model that could be replicated in cities across Africa. Through strategic partnership and a shared commitment to innovation, Zola and Rajesh built something far greater than either could have achieved alone.

Great collaborations don't just solve problems—they create new possibilities.

Key Action Points from Zola's Story

- **Collaboration Drives Innovation:** By teaming up with Rajesh, Zola was able to introduce her solar solutions to a new market and create a more comprehensive product offering.
- **Look Beyond Your Industry:** Sometimes the best solutions come from partnering with those outside of your immediate sector, as Zola did with a real estate developer.
- **Shared Vision Is Key:** Zola and Rajesh's collaboration worked because they shared a common goal of promoting sustainability, which aligned their efforts and made the partnership stronger.
- **Think Big but Start Small:** Zola and Rajesh launched one housing project first to test their collaboration, allowing them to refine their model before scaling.

47. Empowering and Elevating Others to Drive Collective Success

True leadership is not about individual achievement but about empowering others to succeed. When leaders focus on elevating those around them, they foster collaboration, drive collective success, and create a culture of shared purpose. Empowerment leads to stronger teams, better performance, and long-lasting impact.

In the bustling city of Dakar, Senegal, Lamine Touré, a Senegalese-French entrepreneur, had built a successful tech company, "InnovateX," which specialised in developing affordable software solutions for small businesses in West Africa. His goal had always been to make technology accessible for entrepreneurs, helping them grow their businesses and contribute to the local economy. However, as InnovateX grew, Lamine realised that he couldn't achieve his long-term vision alone. He needed to empower his team to take ownership, innovate, and lead in their respective roles.

Lamine's leadership journey wasn't without challenges. Early on, he was involved in every decision, from product development to client management, often feeling like he needed to oversee everything to ensure success. But as the team expanded, it became clear that this hands-on approach was holding the company back. Employees weren't as motivated or confident in their abilities, relying on Lamine to guide every step of the way.

One of Lamine's key team members, Fatima Lee, a Korean-Senegalese software engineer, had tremendous potential, but she was hesitant to take on leadership roles. Lamine recognized that if InnovateX was going to thrive, he needed to change his approach. He decided to empower Fatima and other team members by giving them more autonomy and responsibility. He began with small steps, encouraging Fatima to lead a major client project from start to finish. At first, she was reluctant, unsure if she could meet the high standards Lamine had set for the company.

But Lamine didn't just assign her the task and step away—he supported her with guidance when needed and offered encouragement while giving her the freedom to make decisions. Over time, Fatima gained confidence, and the project turned out to be a huge success. The client was thrilled, and Fatima's leadership on the project was a turning point for her career.

Seeing the impact of empowering his team, Lamine expanded this approach across the company. He initiated mentorship programs, cross-functional training, and open innovation challenges where team members could present new ideas and take ownership of their implementation. As employees began to feel more empowered, InnovateX thrived. Productivity increased, and the company started to innovate faster, introducing products that catered to a broader range of clients.

Lamine's shift from micromanaging to empowering others not only helped InnovateX grow but also fostered a culture where everyone contributed to the company's success. He realised that by investing in the growth and leadership of his team, he was building a stronger, more resilient organisation.

True leadership is about empowering those around you to achieve greatness, together.

Key Action Points from Lamine's Story

- **Empowerment Drives Innovation:** By giving his team more autonomy, Lamine unlocked their potential, leading to new ideas and faster innovation.
- **Leaders Should Support, Not Control:** Lamine's transition from micromanaging to empowering allowed his employees to take ownership of their work and succeed on their own terms.
- **Building Confidence in Others is Key:** By encouraging Fatima to lead, Lamine helped her develop confidence, ultimately strengthening the entire team.
- **Shared Success is Lasting Success:** Lamine's focus on elevating others created a culture of collective achievement, driving long-term growth for InnovateX.

48. The Power of Strategic Foresight to Anticipate Trends Before They Happen

Strategic foresight is the ability to anticipate market trends before they emerge. Leaders who use this skill can position their businesses to capitalise on future opportunities and mitigate risks, giving them a significant advantage in an ever-changing marketplace.

Akua Osei, a Ghanaian-Kenyan entrepreneur, founded "EcoPure," a company specialising in eco-friendly cleaning products. Akua had always been passionate about sustainability and saw an opportunity to create non-toxic, biodegradable cleaning solutions for the African market. While her business was steadily growing, Akua knew that staying ahead of industry trends was key to long-term success.

One day, Akua attended an international sustainability conference in Berlin, where she met Tobias Richter, a German environmental economist. They discussed the future of sustainable products, and Tobias mentioned a growing trend in Europe toward waterless cleaning products due to increasing water scarcity concerns. He advised Akua to consider how this trend might eventually make its way to Africa, especially as water shortages became more common in various regions.

Akua returned to Nairobi with a new perspective.

Although water shortages were not yet a major issue in Kenya, she realised that anticipating this trend could give EcoPure a competitive edge in the future. Akua decided to invest in research and development to create a line of waterless cleaning products, even though the demand wasn't immediate.

Her decision proved to be a masterstroke. Within two years, East Africa began experiencing more severe droughts, and water conservation became a top priority for consumers and businesses alike. By the time this trend fully hit the region, EcoPure was the only company in the market with a waterless cleaning solution. Akua's strategic foresight allowed her to be a first-mover, and EcoPure's sales skyrocketed.

Akua's ability to anticipate market needs before they emerged turned EcoPure into a regional leader in sustainable products. By staying ahead of trends and preparing for future demands, Akua ensured her company's success in a rapidly changing environment.

Strategic foresight isn't about reacting to what's happening now, it's about seeing what's coming next and preparing your business to lead the way.

Key Action Points from Akua's Story

- **Monitor Global Trends:** Akua's strategic foresight came from staying informed about international trends and recognising how they might impact her local market.
- **Invest in Innovation Early:** By developing waterless products before there was widespread demand, Akua positioned EcoPure as a leader when the trend hit.
- **Be a First-Mover:** Akua's decision to act early on emerging trends gave her a significant competitive advantage when the market shifted.
- **Adapt to Long-Term Challenges:** Anticipating future challenges like water scarcity allowed Akua to future-proof her business and stay ahead of competitors.

49. Unlocking Global Opportunities for Growth Beyond Boarders

Expanding into global markets can open up new growth opportunities for businesses. Leaders who are willing to navigate cultural, regulatory, and logistical complexities can tap into larger customer bases, diversify revenue streams, and increase their company's resilience in the face of local market challenges.

In the bustling city of Bridgetown, Barbados, Marise Etienne, a Haitian-Barbadian entrepreneur, founded "CaribWear," a fashion brand specialising in eco-friendly, culturally inspired Caribbean clothing. CaribWear was a hit in the local market, celebrated for its bold designs and commitment to sustainable practices. However, after several years of success, Marise felt that her business had reached a plateau. She knew there was potential for CaribWear beyond the Caribbean, but she wasn't sure how to take her brand global.

While attending a fashion expo in London, Marise met Yuki Nakamura, a Japanese fashion distributor with expertise in global supply chains. Yuki was impressed by CaribWear's unique blend of sustainability and Caribbean culture and believed it would resonate with consumers in Japan, where eco-friendly and artisanal products were becoming increasingly popular. Yuki proposed helping Marise introduce her brand to the Japanese market.

Despite her initial hesitation—after all, Japan seemed far removed from the Caribbean—Marise saw this as an opportunity to expand her brand beyond regional borders. She worked closely with Yuki to adapt CaribWear's marketing strategy to the Japanese market. This involved adjusting the product range to include designs inspired by both Caribbean and Japanese aesthetics and ensuring that the brand's sustainability message aligned with Japan's environmental priorities.

The launch in Japan was a success. CaribWear's fusion of cultures resonated with fashion-forward consumers, and Marise's commitment to sustainable production was a significant selling point in an eco-conscious market. The global expansion not only boosted CaribWear's sales but also raised its profile internationally, leading to new opportunities in Europe and North America.

By embracing global opportunities, Marise unlocked new avenues for growth and transformed CaribWear into a truly international brand. Her willingness to venture beyond borders and adapt her business for different markets set her on a path to sustained success.

Unlocking global opportunities requires more than just ambition. It demands adaptability and the courage to blend cultures and ideas.

Key Action Points from Marise's Story

- **Be Open to Global Partnerships:** Marise's collaboration with Yuki helped her successfully navigate the complexities of entering a new market.
- **Adapt Your Product for New Markets:** By blending Caribbean and Japanese aesthetics, Marise ensured that CaribWear resonated with local consumers.
- **Leverage Global Trends:** Marise capitalised on Japan's growing demand for eco-friendly products, which aligned with CaribWear's sustainability mission.
- **Expand Beyond Local Limitations:** Going global allowed Marise to overcome the limitations of her regional market and achieve significant growth.

50. The Art of Reflection to Learn from Every Chapter in Your Leadership Journey

Leadership is a continuous learning process. Reflection allows leaders to assess their experiences, learn from successes and failures, and adapt for the future. Those who take the time to reflect on each chapter of their journey grow stronger, more insightful, and better equipped to navigate future challenges.

Ebo Ofori, a Ghanaian entrepreneur that moved to Amsterdam, had built "Harvest Foods," a sustainable food company specialising in plant-based products made from ingredients sourced across Africa. His company had gained international recognition for promoting ethical farming and bringing African culinary traditions to the European market. Ebo's business was thriving, but as it expanded, he faced increasingly complex challenges that required him to lead in new ways.

Ebo had always been an action-oriented leader, focused on pushing forward with new ideas and seizing opportunities. However, as Harvest Foods grew, he began to notice patterns in his leadership that weren't serving him well. There were moments when rapid expansion had led to supply chain issues, or times when he had rushed decisions without fully considering the long-term impact. Ebo realised that in order to grow as a leader, he needed to slow down and reflect on the lessons he had learned throughout his journey.

Feeling the need for perspective, Ebo reached out to his friend and colleague, Leila Moradi, an IraSharessen-French business strategist with a talent for helping leaders reflect and recalibrate. During a quiet evening by the Amsterdam canals, Leila asked Ebo a simple but powerful question: "When was the last time you stopped to truly reflect on everything you've accomplished and the lessons learned along the way?"

Ebo thought for a moment and realised that in his drive for progress, he had rarely taken the time to look back. Leila encouraged him to schedule regular reflection sessions—moments where he could assess his leadership, identify key takeaways from each chapter of his journey, and make adjustments for the future.

Inspired by this advice, Ebo began incorporating structured reflection into his leadership routine. He set aside time at the end of each quarter to review his company's progress, assess his personal leadership growth, and analyse decisions that had worked—and those that hadn't. By doing so, Ebo gained a clearer understanding of how his choices shaped the company's direction.

Through reflection, Ebo recognised that his tendency to prioritise growth at all costs had sometimes compromised the company's core values. Moving forward, he made a conscious effort to balance growth with sustainability, ensuring that Harvest Foods maintained its ethical commitments while expanding. He also used these reflections to empower his team, encouraging them to share their own insights and learnings, which fostered a culture of continuous improvement.

The results were profound. Harvest Foods became not only a leader in the sustainable food industry but also a model for how reflection can fuel innovation and growth. Ebo's willingness to learn from each chapter in his leadership journey helped him evolve into a more thoughtful, adaptable, and effective leader.

Leadership isn't just about moving forward, it's about looking back, learning from every chapter, and using those lessons to shape the future.

Key Action Points from Ebo's Story

- **Reflection is Essential for Growth:** Ebo's success came from taking the time to reflect on his leadership journey, learning from both successes and mistakes.
- **Balance Action with Thoughtful Analysis:** While Ebo was action-oriented, reflection helped him slow down and make more thoughtful, long-term decisions.
- **Create a Culture of Learning:** By encouraging his team to reflect and share their learnings, Ebo fostered a culture of continuous improvement within his company.
- **Adapt Through Reflection:** Reflection helped Ebo identify patterns in his leadership, allowing him to make key adjustments that benefited both the company and its values.

51. Rewriting the Playbook and How to Lead When There Are No Rules

In times of uncertainty or when venturing into uncharted territory, there may not be a clear roadmap to follow. Leaders who succeed in these situations are those who have the courage to innovate, trust their instincts, and create new strategies that adapt to ever-changing environments.

Ayodele Mensah, a Senegalese-American entrepreneur, had built her startup, "Digital Pathways," into a leading tech consultancy focused on digital transformation for businesses in West Africa. Ayodele's company helped businesses adopt cutting-edge technologies and navigate the challenges of the digital age. However, when the COVID-19 pandemic struck, businesses across the continent were thrown into disarray, and many of Ayodele's clients were struggling to adapt to a world suddenly dependent on remote work and digital infrastructure.

Ayodele knew that if Digital Pathways was to survive, they needed to help their clients in new, innovative ways. The problem? No one had ever faced a situation like this before—there was no playbook for how to lead businesses through a pandemic-induced digital transformation on such a massive scale. Rather than waiting for solutions to emerge, Ayodele decided it was time to rewrite the rules.

One of her key clients, a large agricultural cooperative in Senegal, was on the brink of collapse due to their inability to operate under lockdown conditions. They needed a way to keep their supply chains running and manage communications across remote teams. Ayodele, inspired by a conversation with her French colleague and systems engineer, Luc Dubois, decided to introduce a groundbreaking virtual platform. This platform would allow the cooperative to digitise its supply chain, track logistics in real-time, and communicate seamlessly with farmers and distributors in even the most remote areas.

It wasn't an easy transition, but Ayodele led the cooperative through it step by step, offering virtual training sessions, on-the-ground support, and constant adjustments to the platform based on real-time feedback from users. What set Ayodele apart was her willingness to embrace the unknown and her ability to think creatively in a crisis. She knew the old methods wouldn't work and trusted her instincts to chart a new course.

Within months, the agricultural cooperative was not only surviving but thriving under the new digital model. The successful transformation became a case study for other businesses across the region, and Digital Pathways grew exponentially as Ayodele's clients saw her as a leader who could guide them through the unknown.

Ayodele didn't just help her clients survive the crisis—she helped them adapt, innovate, and emerge stronger. Her leadership during unprecedented times turned Digital Pathways into a trailblazer in the tech consultancy industry across West Africa.

When there are no rules, leadership is about having the courage to create your own path. Trust your instincts, adapt to the unknown, and lead with confidence.

Key Action Points from Ayodele's Story

- **Embrace the Unknown:** Ayodele's success came from her ability to lead without a roadmap, trusting her instincts and creating new solutions in uncharted territory.
- **Innovate in a Crisis:** When faced with unprecedented challenges, Ayodele's willingness to rewrite the playbook helped her clients survive and thrive.
- **Adapt to Changing Conditions:** By staying flexible and adjusting her strategy based on real-time feedback, Ayodele ensured the success of her digital platform.
- **Lead with Courage and Conviction:** In the absence of clear rules, Ayodele's bold decision-making and belief in her vision inspired confidence in her clients and team.

52. Strategic Storytelling to Build a Narrative That Drives Action

Strategic storytelling is a powerful tool for leaders to inspire, persuade, and motivate others to take action. Crafting a compelling narrative that connects emotionally with your audience and aligns with your goals can drive not only engagement but also tangible results.

Amari Casimir, an African-American entrepreneur with roots in Haiti, was the founder of "Vital Greens," a health food company focused on organic juices and plant-based products. Vital Greens had seen steady growth, but Amari was preparing to launch a new line of products that she believed would elevate her brand to the next level: a range of nutrient-rich juices sourced from organic farms across the Caribbean, highlighting the richness of the region's natural ingredients.

However, as the launch date approached, Amari faced an unexpected challenge. Her marketing campaign wasn't generating the buzz she had hoped for, and her sales team reported lukewarm responses from retailers. The Caribbean-sourced product line, while innovative, wasn't resonating with the target market. Amari knew that something had to change if she wanted her new line to be a success.

Frustrated but determined, Amari reached out to her friend and mentor, Sofia Rivera, a marketing expert from Argentina, for advice. Sofia immediately identified the issue: the marketing campaign was focused too much on the product's features and not enough on its story. "Amari, you're selling something much bigger than juice," Sofia said. "You're selling a connection—to culture, to the land, to a healthier way of life. You need to tell that story."

Inspired by Sofia's words, Amari shifted her approach. Rather than focusing solely on the product itself, she crafted a strategic narrative around the origins of Vital Greens' new line. The story highlighted the vibrant communities of farmers in Haiti, Jamaica, and Barbados, whose sustainable farming practices were rooted in generations of tradition. The narrative also tied back to Amari's own heritage, sharing her journey as a Haitian-American entrepreneur and her mission to bring the vitality of the Caribbean to the world through health-conscious products.

Amari's team produced visually stunning marketing materials that showcased the lush, green landscapes of the Caribbean, accompanied by stories of the farmers who grew the ingredients. She also hosted community events, where customers could taste the products while learning about the positive social and environmental impact of supporting organic Caribbean farms.

The narrative resonated deeply with customers. Suddenly, it wasn't just about buying a juice—it was about supporting sustainable agriculture, embracing Caribbean culture, and becoming part of a broader mission for healthier living. Retailers took notice, and Vital Greens' new product line began flying off the shelves.

By strategically telling a story that connected with the emotions and values of her audience, Amari turned a slow start into a wildly successful product launch. Her storytelling not only boosted sales but also strengthened the brand's identity, turning Vital Greens into a movement for conscious consumption.

The power of a story lies in its ability to connect, inspire, and move people to action.

Key Action Points from Amari's Story

- **Focus on the Story, Not Just the Product:** Amari's shift from promoting product features to crafting a compelling narrative was the key to her successful launch.
- **Connect Emotionally with Your Audience:** By sharing her personal journey and the cultural significance of her products, Amari created a deeper connection with her customers.
- **Use Visual Storytelling to Enhance Impact:** The visually rich marketing materials brought Amari's story to life and helped customers visualise the values behind the product.
- **Align Your Narrative with Your Mission:** Amari's story wasn't just about selling juice—it was about aligning her brand with a mission of sustainability, culture, and health.

53. Building Legacy Leadership and Leading with a Future-First Mindset

Legacy leadership is about more than achieving short-term success—it's about creating a lasting impact that will endure long after you're gone. Leaders who think beyond the present, focusing on the long-term sustainability of their business, create a legacy that can inspire future generations.

In the rapidly evolving city of Accra, Ghana, Kwesi Bediako, a Ghanaian-British entrepreneur, founded "FutureWave," an innovative education technology company focused on equipping young Africans with the skills they needed to thrive in a digital future. The company offered online courses in coding, artificial intelligence, and entrepreneurship, providing access to cutting-edge education for students in underserved areas.

Kwesi was passionate about the mission of FutureWave, but as the company grew, he faced increasing pressure from investors to scale quickly and maximise short-term profits. There was immense demand for his services, and while scaling too fast would generate immediate financial gains, Kwesi worried it might compromise the quality of education and the long-term impact he envisioned. He had always wanted FutureWave to be more than just a business; he wanted it to leave a legacy of empowerment and innovation across the continent.

Feeling conflicted, Kwesi turned to his friend, Sara Gupta, an Indian-American social entrepreneur based in Nairobi, Kenya. Sara had built her own organisation on the principle of legacy leadership, and Kwesi knew she would offer valuable insight. Over a late-night conversation, Sara encouraged Kwesi to stay true to his vision. "Kwesi," she said, "building something that lasts isn't about how fast you can grow, but about the foundation you set. The decisions you make today will shape FutureWave's legacy for generations to come."

Inspired by Sara's words, Kwesi decided to take a different approach. Rather than chasing rapid growth, he focused on creating a scalable, sustainable model that prioritised quality over quantity. He reinvested in his company's infrastructure, improving the curriculum and expanding teacher training programs to ensure that every student received a world-class education. Kwesi also established partnerships with African universities and international tech companies, creating a pipeline for students to gain practical experience and job placements.

Kwesi's focus on legacy leadership began to pay off. While FutureWave grew at a slower pace than some competitors, it quickly became known for its commitment to excellence and its transformative impact on students' lives. As graduates of FutureWave's programs went on to start their own companies and work for global tech firms, the company's reputation soared. More importantly, Kwesi's vision of creating a lasting legacy for Africa's future leaders was taking shape.

By leading with a future-first mindset, Kwesi ensured that FutureWave wasn't just a passing trend but a movement that would inspire and empower generations of young Africans to dream bigger and achieve more.

When you lead with the future in mind, you create a path for others to follow.

Key Action Points from Kwesi's Story

- **Prioritise Long-Term Impact Over Short-Term Gains:** Kwesi's decision to focus on sustainable growth ensured that FutureWave built a strong foundation for the future.
- **Invest in Quality and Infrastructure:** By reinvesting in teacher training and improving the curriculum, Kwesi created a high-quality education platform that set FutureWave apart.
- **Build Strategic Partnerships for Lasting Impact:** Kwesi's collaborations with universities and tech companies helped bridge the gap between education and employment, creating opportunities for his students.
- **Stay True to Your Vision:** Even in the face of pressure to scale quickly, Kwesi remained committed to his long-term vision, ensuring that FutureWave's legacy would endure.

54. The Art of Graceful Leadership to Balance Strength with Compassion

True leadership requires the ability to balance strength with compassion. A leader must be decisive and firm, but they should also cultivate empathy and understanding. Leaders who can exhibit both qualities earn respect, loyalty, and trust, fostering a culture where people feel empowered to give their best.

Sade Falade, a Nigerian-British professional, was the CEO of "ThriveWell," a fast-growing wellness and mental health tech company that provided digital mental health resources for corporate clients. Under Sade's leadership, ThriveWell had gained significant traction, securing major contracts with leading firms across the UK and Europe. Sade was known for her strong, no-nonsense approach, which had helped the company grow quickly and establish itself as a leader in the corporate wellness industry.

However, as the company expanded, Sade noticed an alarming trend: employee burnout. Several team members had come forward with concerns about the pressure they were under, and some had even left the company due to the high-stress environment. Sade had built ThriveWell with a focus on mental health, yet the very culture within her own company was becoming counterproductive to its mission.

Feeling a personal sense of failure, Sade reached out to her colleague, Luis Hernandez, a Mexican-American leadership coach, for guidance. Luis had a reputation for helping executives find balance in their leadership styles. Over coffee, Sade admitted that while she had driven the company to success with a strong hand, she now realised that her approach lacked the compassion needed to maintain a healthy and supportive workplace.

Luis offered Sade a simple yet profound piece of advice: "Leadership is about more than strength; it's about grace. People need to know that you care as much as you expect. If you balance your strength with compassion, your team will work harder because they feel supported, not just driven."

Inspired by Luis's words, Sade set out to reshape her leadership style. She began by implementing a more flexible work environment, allowing employees to take mental health days and encouraging open communication about workload pressures. Sade also held regular one-on-one meetings with her team, not just to discuss performance but to check in on their well-being. She created a culture where employees felt they could voice concerns without fear of judgement or retribution.

Sade's approach paid off. Employee morale improved, and the rate of burnout significantly decreased. The culture shift also fostered greater innovation, as team members felt empowered to take creative risks, knowing they had a leader who genuinely cared about their growth and well-being. ThriveWell continued to grow, but this time, it was with a renewed sense of purpose and balance.

Through her evolution as a leader, Sade learned that strength and compassion were not opposing forces—they could work in harmony to create a more effective, supportive, and resilient organisation.

Leadership is not just about being strong, it's about being compassionate.

Key Action Points from Sade's Story

- **Strength and Compassion Must Coexist:** Sade's ability to lead with both decisiveness and empathy allowed her to create a healthier and more productive workplace.
- **Foster Open Communication:** By encouraging her team to discuss their challenges and concerns openly, Sade built a culture of trust and transparency.
- **Prioritise Employee Well-Being:** Sade's focus on mental health and flexible work environments helped reduce burnout and improve morale.
- **Leadership is About Care and Expectation:** Sade learned that employees work best when they know their leader cares as much about their well-being as they do about their performance.

55. Unlocking the Power of Ecosystems to Leverage Partnerships for Growth

Business ecosystems provide powerful opportunities for growth by leveraging partnerships. Companies that build strategic alliances can accelerate innovation, access new markets, and scale faster than they could on their own. Collaboration within a network of partners often leads to exponential growth, benefiting all involved.

Ade Oladipo, an entrepreneur, founded "AgriConnect," a digital platform designed to connect small-scale farmers with buyers across Nigeria. Ade had a strong vision: to use technology to bridge the gap between rural farmers and urban markets, making agriculture more profitable and sustainable. AgriConnect had an impressive start, gaining traction locally with a small network of farmers and buyers. However, Ade quickly realised that the platform's growth was limited by the company's resources and reach. To scale up and create a true impact, AgriConnect needed more than just individual growth—it needed to tap into a broader ecosystem.

One evening, while attending a tech conference in Nairobi, Kenya, Ade met Amina Omar, a Kenyan entrepreneur who had built a successful logistics company specialising in delivering goods to remote areas. Amina's company had a robust infrastructure, including partnerships with delivery companies across East Africa. As the two discussed their businesses, Ade recognised the potential for a powerful partnership. By combining AgriConnect's digital platform with Amina's logistics network, they could create a seamless farm-to-market supply chain, ensuring farmers could get their goods to urban markets quickly and efficiently.

Excited about the possibilities, Ade and Amina worked together to create a pilot project, integrating their services. The results were immediate: AgriConnect's farmers could access buyers not only in Lagos but also in Nairobi, Mombasa, and other key cities across East Africa. The logistics support meant that farmers could now expand their reach, while urban buyers benefited from more diverse and fresh produce.

Word of the success spread, and soon, other players in the agricultural ecosystem wanted to join the partnership. Microfinance institutions came on board, offering small loans to farmers to help them scale their production. Agricultural research institutes contributed expertise on crop management and sustainability, improving yields and profitability for farmers. What started as a simple digital platform had now become a thriving ecosystem, with partners across the agriculture, finance, and logistics sectors working together.

Within two years, AgriConnect grew exponentially, expanding its operations beyond Nigeria and into East and West Africa. By leveraging partnerships, Ade was able to scale AgriConnect far beyond what would have been possible alone, unlocking exponential growth through the power of the ecosystem.

When you tap into the power of partnerships, you unlock the potential for exponential growth that benefits not just your business, but everyone in the ecosystem.

Key Action Points from Ade's Story

- **Partnerships Accelerate Growth:** By collaborating with Amina's logistics network, Ade was able to scale AgriConnect quickly and efficiently.
- **Ecosystems Create Value for All:** The partnership not only benefited Ade's business but also improved outcomes for farmers, buyers, and logistics providers, creating a win-win situation.
- **Collaboration Leads to Innovation:** By partnering with diverse organisations, AgriConnect was able to offer new services and improve its platform, driving innovation.
- **Build Strategic Alliances for Long-Term Success:** Ade's ability to build a broad network of partners helped ensure AgriConnect's success and positioned the company for long-term sustainability.

56. Building Resilience for Sustained Success in Business

Sustained success doesn't come from short bursts of effort or rapid wins; it's about building resilience over time. Leaders who focus on the long game, navigating setbacks with perseverance, adaptability, and a clear vision, are the ones who endure and thrive in the face of challenges.

Dakarai Mensah, a South African entrepreneur, had built his startup, "EcoFresh," from a small organic farming business into one of the leading suppliers of sustainable, locally sourced produce in the region. Dakarai had always been passionate about agriculture and food security, and he built EcoFresh with the goal of creating a supply chain that supported local farmers while delivering fresh, eco-friendly produce to consumers across South Africa.

In the early years, EcoFresh grew rapidly, gaining major contracts with restaurants and supermarkets. But just as Dakarai was ready to expand nationwide, the company hit a major obstacle. A severe drought struck South Africa, dramatically reducing crop yields and pushing small farmers to the brink of collapse. The supply chain Dakarai had worked so hard to build was suddenly at risk, and many of his suppliers were struggling to survive. For months, EcoFresh's deliveries slowed to a trickle, and contracts were in jeopardy.

Feeling the weight of the situation, Dakarai sought advice from his mentor, Alicia Vega, a Mexican businesswoman with extensive experience in agricultural innovation. She had successfully guided her own company through challenging conditions in Latin America and knew the importance of resilience in agriculture.

"Dakarai," she said, "in the long game, it's not just about growing when the sun is shining. It's about surviving the storms. You have to be prepared to adapt, change course, and support your foundation—your farmers—if you want EcoFresh to endure."

Inspired by Alicia's words, Dakarai realised that the future of his business depended on building resilience, not just for EcoFresh, but for the entire ecosystem it relied on. Instead of pushing for quick recovery, Dakarai pivoted his strategy.

He invested in water-efficient technologies and collaborated with agricultural experts to introduce drought-resistant crops to his network of farmers. He also formed partnerships with local universities, creating research programs focused on sustainable farming in arid conditions.

Dakarai took a financial hit in the short term, scaling back operations to ensure that his core farmers could survive the drought. But over time, these efforts paid off. EcoFresh's network of farmers became more resilient, and when the drought finally lifted, the company emerged stronger and more sustainable than ever.

With his newfound resilience strategy, Dakarai not only regained his contracts but expanded EcoFresh's reach across South Africa and into neighbouring countries. His ability to play the long game, investing in the future rather than focusing on short-term profits, solidified EcoFresh as a leader in sustainable agriculture.

Build resilience, and you'll win the long game.

Key Action Points from Dakarai's Story

- **Resilience is Built Over Time:** Dakarai's success came from his ability to focus on the long-term sustainability of his business, rather than chasing short-term wins.
- **Adaptability is Key to Surviving Setbacks:** By pivoting his strategy and investing in sustainable farming practices, Dakarai was able to navigate the drought and protect his business.
- **Support Your Foundation:** Dakarai's decision to invest in his network of farmers ensured that EcoFresh's supply chain could withstand future challenges.
- **Long-Term Success Requires Patience:** Dakarai accepted short-term financial losses in order to build a stronger, more resilient business for the future.

57. How Small Wins Lead to Big Breakthroughs with the Multiplier Effect

Success is often built on a series of small wins that, when combined, create a multiplier effect leading to big breakthroughs. Leaders who recognize and leverage these incremental victories can build momentum, driving their teams and businesses toward significant achievements.

Judeline St. Pierre, a Haitian-Canadian entrepreneur, had founded "GreenPulse," a tech startup that specialised in creating energy-efficient solutions for urban environments. GreenPulse's goal was ambitious: to revolutionise how cities consumed energy by developing smart technology for buildings, reducing waste and cutting carbon emissions. While the idea had great potential, GreenPulse faced an uphill battle in its early days. Competing against established companies with much larger budgets, Judeline's team struggled to get attention from major investors and city planners.

But Judeline believed in the power of small wins. She knew that building a sustainable business required patience and a focus on each incremental success. After months of hard work, GreenPulse landed its first small contract with a local university, where they implemented their energy-saving systems in a few campus buildings. It wasn't a major deal, but it was a start.

Judeline celebrated this win with her team, knowing that it could be a stepping stone to bigger things. With the project completed successfully, the university saw immediate improvements in energy efficiency, saving money and reducing their carbon footprint. Judeline used this as a case study, sharing the results with other institutions and pitching GreenPulse's technology to small businesses across Toronto.

Soon after, GreenPulse won a contract with a chain of eco-conscious hotels, implementing their energy systems in multiple locations. Each new project was a small victory, but Judeline was careful to build on every success. With each project, GreenPulse refined its technology, making it more efficient and scalable. These wins started to add up, creating a ripple effect.

While attending a sustainable energy conference in Vancouver, Judeline met Javier Morales, a Spanish urban planner working on green initiatives for cities in Latin America. Javier was impressed by GreenPulse's growing portfolio of successful projects. After discussing Judeline's vision and learning about her previous wins, Javier introduced GreenPulse to city officials in Santiago, Chile, who were looking for ways to reduce energy consumption across government buildings.

This opportunity was the breakthrough Judeline had been working toward. Thanks to the small victories that had built GreenPulse's reputation, the company secured its first international contract, leading a multi-million-dollar energy transformation project in Santiago. This success opened doors across Latin America, and GreenPulse became a recognised leader in sustainable urban energy solutions.

By focusing on small wins and leveraging each one, Judeline had built the momentum that ultimately led to big breakthroughs for her company.

Big breakthroughs are often the result of small wins multiplied over time. Celebrate every victory, because it's the foundation of your future success.

Key Action Points from Judeline's Story

- **Small Wins Create Momentum:** Each project Judeline secured, no matter how small, helped build GreenPulse's credibility and expertise, leading to bigger opportunities.
- **Leverage Every Success:** Judeline used each victory as a case study to attract more clients, showing that even small successes can open new doors.
- **Patience and Persistence Pay Off:** Judeline didn't rush toward big contracts; she built her business slowly and carefully, ensuring long-term growth.
- **Celebrate Small Wins with Your Team:** Acknowledging small victories kept Judeline's team motivated and focused on the bigger picture.

58. Unleashing the Power of Influence to Lead Without Authority

Leadership isn't just about holding a position of authority—it's about influence. The ability to lead and inspire others without formal power requires trust, emotional intelligence, and clear communication. Those who master the art of influence can lead from any position, fostering collaboration and driving success.

Dieynaba Diallo, a Senegalese professional, worked as a senior project manager for a large tech company that specialised in artificial intelligence (AI) solutions. While Dieynaba wasn't in a formal leadership role, she was often called upon to lead cross-functional teams on complex projects. One such project involved developing a groundbreaking AI tool for a major client in the healthcare industry. The stakes were high, and the team she was leading consisted of engineers, marketers, and external stakeholders—many of whom did not report directly to her.

Despite the lack of direct authority, Dieynaba was determined to bring the team together and deliver the project successfully. She knew that the key to success wasn't about issuing orders but about influencing her colleagues and creating a shared sense of purpose.

Dieynaba's first challenge came when a key engineer, Anwar, a Syrian-born AI specialist, hesitated to prioritise the project. He had other competing tasks, and since Dieynaba wasn't his direct supervisor, he didn't feel a strong obligation to focus on her initiative. Instead of trying to push or demand his attention, Dieynaba took a different approach. She invited Anwar for coffee, where they discussed the project's potential impact on healthcare—how the AI tool they were building could revolutionise patient care and make diagnoses faster and more accurate.

Dieynaba shared her passion for the project and listened intently to Anwar's thoughts. She made him feel valued, asking for his input on how they could improve the tool's capabilities. Her enthusiasm and respect for his expertise sparked a change. Anwar began to see the project not as just another task, but as an opportunity to be part of something impactful. He committed his full attention to the project and became one of its strongest advocates.

Dieynaba applied this same strategy with the marketing team and external stakeholders. Through clear communication, empathy, and an ability to connect with others on a personal level, she earned their trust and commitment without ever needing formal authority.

The result? The project was completed ahead of schedule, with innovative features that exceeded the client's expectations. Dieynaba's ability to influence, rather than command, had transformed a group of disconnected individuals into a high-performing, collaborative team.

Her leadership style demonstrated the power of influence, and her reputation within the company grew, leading to a formal promotion into a leadership role soon after.

Leadership isn't about the authority you have, it's about the influence you wield to empower others.

Key Action Points from Dieynaba's Story

- **Influence Through Passion and Purpose:** Dieynaba inspired her team by sharing her vision for the project and showing how their work would make a real-world impact.
- **Build Trust Through Listening:** Dieynaba's willingness to listen and value her colleagues' expertise built trust and commitment, even without formal authority.
- **Empathy is Key to Leading Without Power:** Dieynaba's empathetic approach, understanding her colleagues' challenges, helped her influence them more effectively than issuing demands.
- **Leadership Comes From Actions, Not Titles:** Dieynaba demonstrated that leadership is about behaviour—communicating, inspiring, and fostering collaboration—rather than holding a title.

59. Finding Your Strategic North Star for the Guiding Principles of Longterm Success

A business's long-term success relies on identifying and following a strategic North Star—a clear guiding principle that shapes decisions, actions, and direction. Leaders who stay aligned with this vision can navigate challenges, adapt to change, and build a resilient organisation that endures over time.

Bintou Diarra, a Black French-Malian entrepreneur, had founded "Etoile Santé," a health-tech company aimed at making personalised healthcare accessible to underserved communities across Europe. Etoile Santé's technology allowed patients to monitor their health and connect with medical professionals remotely. Bintou's passion for healthcare stemmed from her own experiences growing up in Mali, where access to quality healthcare was limited. She was determined to bridge that gap with innovative technology.

In the early stages of the company, Bintou was faced with many tempting opportunities to grow quickly. Investors wanted her to pivot the business model toward wealthier markets where there was more money to be made, and some even suggested focusing on luxury health services for high-paying clients. These changes could have brought in quick returns, but Bintou felt uneasy about straying from her original mission: to provide affordable, high-quality healthcare for underserved communities. She knew that chasing short-term profits would take Etoile Santé away from its true purpose.

Bintou reached out to her mentor, Javier Fernandez, a Spanish social entrepreneur she had met while studying in Madrid. Javier had built a successful nonprofit in the healthcare sector and understood the challenges of staying committed to a vision when there were easier paths to immediate financial success. Over a long conversation, Javier reminded Bintou that businesses, like stars, need a North Star to guide them. "The market will always try to pull you in different directions," Javier said, "but if you stay true to your North Star—the guiding principle that drives you—you will build something lasting."

With Javier's advice in mind, Bintou made the difficult decision to turn down the offers that would have diluted Etoile Santé's mission. Instead, she chose to focus on expanding the company's reach into underserved areas of France, where access to healthcare was limited. She also worked on developing partnerships with local governments and NGOs, keeping Etoile Santé's services affordable and aligned with its core values.

It wasn't an easy road. The company grew slower than it would have if Bintou had taken the more lucrative route, but her commitment to her North Star paid off in the long term. As the healthcare crisis in Europe deepened, Etoile Santé's focus on providing equitable healthcare to underserved communities gained widespread recognition. The French government eventually partnered with Etoile Santé to roll out its services nationwide, expanding access to millions of people.

Through the ups and downs, Bintou's decision to stay true to her guiding principle allowed Etoile Santé to achieve its long-term goal of transforming healthcare for those who needed it most.

Your North Star is your guiding principle, stay true to it, no matter the challenges or distractions.

Key Action Points from Bintou's Story

- **Identify Your North Star:** Bintou's success came from having a clear guiding principle—making healthcare accessible to underserved communities—and staying aligned with it.
- **Resist the Temptation of Short-Term Gains:** By turning down offers that didn't align with her mission, Bintou avoided distractions and focused on long-term success.
- **Partnerships Aligned with Values Lead to Growth:** Bintou's partnerships with governments and NGOs helped her scale Etoile Santé while maintaining her mission.
- **Staying True to Your Vision Pays Off:** Although Bintou faced slower growth, her commitment to her strategic North Star led to long-term recognition and success.

Be Part of Black Rise

Black Rise is a powerful platform dedicated to uplifting Black professionals and entrepreneurs by connecting them with global opportunities, networks, and resources. Our mission is to create a world where economic equity is not just a goal, but a reality. Whether you're a seasoned business owner, an entrepreneur, an experienced professional or just starting your professional journey, Black Rise offers you the network, tools, support, and community to help you thrive.

By joining Black Rise, you'll gain access to:
- A growing global community of like-minded individuals focused on economic empowerment.
- Exclusive events, workshops, and resources tailored to help you succeed.
- Opportunities to connect with potential collaborators,
- investors, and mentors.
- Insights and advice from industry leaders and successful entrepreneurs.

Scan the QR code or visit www.theblackrise.com to join us today. Take the next step in your journey, and be part of a movement dedicated to collective progress and economic success.

Together, we rise!

Thank you

Flavilla Fongang

The founder of Black Rise

www.ingramcontent.com/pod-product-compliance
Lightning Source LLC
Chambersburg PA
CBHW051530240526
45471CB00019B/315